ROOTED IN IRON AND ICE

ROOTED IN IRON AND ICE

INNOCENT YEARS ON THE MESABI

by

Gary W. Barfknecht

NORTH STAR PRESS OF ST. CLOUD, INC.

St. Cloud, Minnesota

ISBN 978-0-87839-746-4

First Edition: March 2014

Published in the United States of America

Published by
North Star Press of St. Cloud, Inc.
P.O. Box 451
St. Cloud, Minnesota 56302

northstarpress.com

My fondest boyhood memories are of time spent with my grandfather,

Paul H. Barfknecht

And though I am now older than he was when he died,

I still miss him.

Paul H. and Gary W. (Author's collection)

Contents

Preface

I LEFT HOME AT AGE EIGHTEEN.

But I stayed in contemporary touch by visiting regularly. And I connected with my past by sharing the circumstances and experiences of my youth with family, friends, and associates. They often reacted with head-shaking disbelief, sometimes even remarking that my stories must be exaggerated, maybe even made up.

The reaction was so consistent, so many times, for so long that I decided my childhood was unusual and, yes, even sometimes unbelievable enough to widely share.

Please enjoy and, yeah, maybe shake your head at the following collection of recollections about my formative years during a singular era, in a place unlike any other. They *are* all true.

To the best of my recollection.

Canada

Mesabi Iron Range

Lake
Superior

Duluth

Minneapolis

Wisconsin

M I N N E S O T A

Introduction

In Place, Out of Time

JUST MONTHS BEFORE THE APPROACHING baby-boom tsunami, I emerged from the gene pool into Minnesota's Mesabi Iron Range. The evolutionary assignment to that frigid, isolated, inhospitable strip of mineral wealth ensured that my childhood would bear little resemblance to that of budding boomers on the outside. In effect, homes on my Range comprised a small, insular foreign country, with its own culture, language, and one-of-a-kind terrain. The problems, pressures, and pleasures that shaped other post-World War II kids rarely crossed our borders. And the outside world's rules and restrictions didn't apply.

The two- to ten-mile-wide spine of the Mesabi jogs, twists and turns from northeast Minnesota's distinct "Arrowhead" region 110 miles to the southwest. Concentrated in that ribbon of real estate was the world's largest body of iron ore. Eastern U.S. corporations and climate controlled removal of the red riches and dominated and defined the area and its people.

Prehistoric geological forces deposited basins of high-grade hematite throughout the Mesabi. Beginning in the 1890s, men and machines scooped out the ancient ore by the millions of tons, creating terraced canyons called "pits." Unusable rock was piled into extensive flat-topped ridges called "dumps." Cities, villages, and company-controlled "locations" perched at the edges of the gaping holes and snuggled up to the man-made mesas. Many of the settlements were transitory. Mining corporations routinely displaced or demolished them to get at the ore beneath.

Mined ore was pulverized by metal-monolith "crushers," then funneled into a procession of railroad cars that rumbled to Lake Superior ports. At immense docks there, the trains dumped their loads into the cavernous bowels of 600-foot-long, 15,000-ton freighters that squeezed through Michigan's Soo Locks then unloaded their cargo at eastern Great Lakes mills. After a blast-furnace fusion with charred coal and limestone, Mesabi ore traveled as steel to the far reaches of the country and globe.

It was a long journey because, even as other Minnesotans joked, though the Range wasn't exactly at the end of the world, you could see it from there.

And that humorous hyperbole came closest to reality from my childhood vantage point, the Ridgewood addition to Virginia, "Queen City of the Iron Range." Swampland slogged south nearly sixty miles, with few inhabited interruptions. Stretching north and east were millions of acres of boreal forest splashed with thousands of pristine lakes, much of which were or would be designated as state, national, and provincial wilderness parks. Just minutes from the Queen City, you could put in a canoe and paddle and portage through 700 miles of wilderness to Canada's Hudson Bay.

But you wouldn't have much time to do it, because equal to mining in forging the character of Rangers were the long, white, brutally cold winters. Snow often began falling by Halloween and sometimes didn't stop until layering a final few inches to a foot and a half in May. Annual mean temperature at Virginia was a few degrees above freezing. January average temperatures rarely rose above zero. And on a few savage nights, almost all thermometer alcohol dove into the bulb below the minus-fifty mark.

During winters, frozen pits and shipping lanes forced mining operations to a near-halt. Laid-off miners either found other work or lined up for public-assistance checks. When pits and ports thawed, ore usually moved again, but not guaranteed. When recessions reduced demand for steel and, therefore, iron, mines shut down. And when miners collectively determined that working conditions had deteriorated to intolerable or wages exploitive, they halted operations through strikes.

No Ranger eluded nature's assaults, and few could avoid the vagaries of mining. So most adults comprised an implicit alliance against climate and corporate control. And they presented a uniform front. Everyone was Everyman. But everyone was also expected to be independent and self-reliant. The result was a pervasive sameness without symmetry.

The consistency wrapped me in stability and security. I knew what to expect and what was expected of me. There were few complexities and no subtleties to

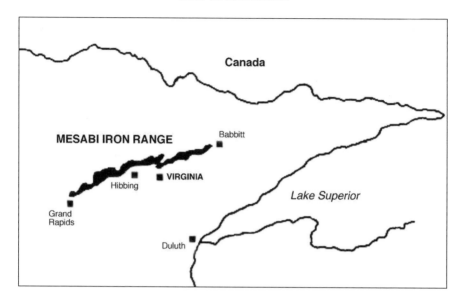

confuse me. Adults rarely intervened, but if needed, I could count on their help. I wandered my neighborhood then city with few restrictions, unsupervised by anyone but under the watchful eyes of everyone. My boundaries gradually expanded, and the surrounding wilderness became a limitless recreation area.

But during the winter, I focused free time on a natural outdoor ice rink directly across the street from our house. And though it and a dozen others throughout town melted into summer playgrounds, we played few traditional and no organized sports there, instead opting or forced to improvise.

Even mines, for instance, were illicitly used for fun by kids who lived near them. They scaled the pits' terraced walls, or used off-duty railroad cars, trucks, and other monstrous equipment as giant jungle gyms. The most-daring practiced cliff diving into abandoned pits—some hundreds of feet deep—that had filled with water. And in winter, the steep sides of dumps turned into runs for anything that would slide.

Kid life was not universally idyllic or benign, however. Our toes and ears regularly and painfully froze. Head cracks onto ice were as common as colds and treated with the same degree of concern. We active boys also risked damaging teeth and noses, often from hockey sticks and pucks but also fists, since fighting was the form of conflict resolution most accepted, endorsed, even encouraged by adults.

3

But our bad breaks didn't break our parents' budgets. Labor-negotiated insurance provided near-complete dental and medical care from cradle to grave for miners and their families. And in the Queen City, that meant potentially at the hands of one physician. My pediatrician also served as county coroner.

Taxes levied on mining companies also ensured that we attended some of the state's finest schools. The outwardly austere, multi-story edifices were gilded with marble floors, ornate chandeliers, commissioned murals, oak doors and trim, and gymnasiums. The junior-high and high-school buildings both additionally housed regulation, multi-lane swimming pools. And just about all of the city's plays, concerts, and other performances were staged at an elegant, 1,100-seat auditorium, including a balcony, also in the junior high.

Our schools were also staffed by disciplined educators who dispensed excellent, no-frills education in the basic three-R's. Curiosity, creativity, and critical thinking, however, were largely ignored, even discouraged.

Teachers who came from the outside also tried to modify our peculiar way of speaking. When mining exploded on the Range around the turn of the twentieth century, the tremendous need for laborers attracted tens of thousands of immigrants from more than forty different ethnic backgrounds. Probably nowhere else on earth had so many different tongues been so quickly compressed into such a small area. The resulting Babel inflected Range speech with a dialect so distinct that, outside our borders, it provoked curiosity, sometimes ridicule.

But that didn't bother me, because I rarely left my neighborhood, let alone the Queen City or the Range. I didn't care about anything that was happening on the outside, because I didn't know that anything else was happening.

I was on my own, but not alone.

Separation Anxiety

I WAS STANDARD-ISSUED, but not under or into standard circumstances.

Several hours after I had insisted on leaving Mom's womb, she finally released me into the experienced hands of Doctor H.E. Rokala at 5:11 a.m. on March 15, 1945. After passing me off to nurse Brooks, Dr. Rokala signed my official admission ticket to life: birth certificate #82. Meanwhile, Brooks lowered me into a wheeled crib and attached a blue tag provided compliments of Nestle's Lion Brand Evaporated Milk. On it she had penciled my name, Gary, chosen to commemorate an uncle who had died five years before, at age three, from complications due to measles. My rolling route to the nursery, on the second floor of Virginia's municipal hospital, included a brief stop to allow—with neither my nor my mother's consent—the hospital's pediatrician to slice off and discard my penis foreskin.

While I protested loudly, Mom lay near-numb from a more-devastating loss. Just five days before, the War Department had notified her that her soldier-husband, my father, Walter, had died in rural France. Exactly two years from the day of his induction, a .30-caliber bullet had slammed into Walter's abdomen shortly after he had returned from a tiny church near the French farmer with whom he was billeted. Adding to Mom's anguish, one of Walt's own squad members, a fellow-draftee from the Range, had accidentally fired the fatal shot. Western Union had delivered the shock, but with a morbid mixup. War Department policy specified that two telegrams be sent in sequence. The first was intended to prepare survivors by prevaricating, "Your husband has been wounded in action." A couple of days later, a "We regret to inform you your husband has died" followed. Mom received the messages in reverse order.

Walter Barfknecht, 1944.
(Author collection)

So there we lay on a cold, rainy, gloomy morning, enduring our pain separately together, but comforted by a large presence. When Walt had received his orders for overseas duty, Mom's parents, in Duluth, informed her that, though they thought it nice she was pregnant with her first child, there was no room for us in their otherwise-empty home and apparently hearts. So immediately after Walt shipped out, his folks, Paul and Mabel Barfknecht, had taken Mom into their rented house, in the company of their two youngest children. Conveniently, the hospital was only six blocks away.

When Mom began experiencing sensations she didn't comprehend, Mabel, having launched six lives, did. So shortly before midnight, she urged Mom onto the front seat of their '41 Mercury. She then somehow maneuvered the 300-pounds of flesh that sagged from her five-foot, one-inch body into the back seat, and Paul drove to the hospital. He then continued on to his night shift at the U.S. Steel-owned Oliver iron mine. Mabel stayed, serving as a soft bed rail until Paul returned and took her home a few hours after my birth.

As was the way of the time in the Queen City, though neither Mom nor I had experienced any complications, we were sentenced to a week and a half in the hospital. On day one, postpartum policy allowed Mom to briefly sit up in bed and dangle her feet, and she was not permitted to become ambulatory for another four days. Initially, nurses brought me in only for twice-a-day feedings, but then Mom's and my time together gradually increased until we were released to Grandma and Grandpa B.

My first stint in the Queen City was brief, but so was the following furlough. We lived with the Barfknechts four months, then relocated sixty-five miles south to Duluth. There, we moved in with Mom's older, sole sister, Catherine, and her husband, Sam Hedberg, who had used our situation as motivation out of their small, rented apartment and into a purchased home. While with them, we made trips north for reunions with Grandma and Grandpa B.

During one visit, a day after my first birthday, we attended the wedding of Phyllis Stoltz, the oldest daughter of Barfknecht-family friends. Also in attendance was Howard, one of the bride's five brothers. Mom had previously met Howard when, shortly after she had moved in with the Barfknechts, they had invited the Stoltz family, including Howard, to dinner. Walter had just left for the war, and Howard had just returned—on crutches—after sleeping more

Howard and Lucille Stoltz. Wedding, 1947. (Author collection)

than a thousand nights in one-man foxholes as he battled through combat zones on two continents.

Born three months after the World War I ending armistice and drafted in 1941 out of his shovel-running job in the iron mines, Howard had landed in Oran, Africa, as part of an anti-aircraft unit. His contingent then thundered through Algiers and Tunis before cruising on landing craft across the Mediterranean Sea to Italy. Near the Leaning Tower of Pisa in the spring of 1944, he and his comrades were unexpectedly ordered to become infantrymen. They abandoned their trailer-mounted .50-caliber machine guns in the surrounding forest and shouldered individual M-1 rifles. For the next four months, he trudged, crouched and belly-crawled beneath enemy fire into southern France.

In Dijon, September 1944, as Howard searched a recently bombed hangar for usable instruments and equipment, he stepped on live, high-tension wires hidden by debris. The current seared flesh off his lower left leg and painfully ended his tour. He was evacuated and flown stateside where, after his medical transport plane made an emergency landing in a farm field, he spent four excruciating months receiving skin grafts while rehabilitating in southeastern U.S. Army hospitals. Finally, he returned to his family's Queen City home and mine employment.

During the year following Phyllis's wedding, Mom's visits to Virginia included more-frequent and involved time with Howard. And Howard regularly motorvated down US-53 to Duluth in the like-new '41 Chev he had put up on blocks during his service years. Finally, he issued a sincere, backdoor proposal to Lucille: "I really like Gary a lot, and I'd like to have him around all the time. Would you mind coming along with the deal?"

In a Baptist minister's living room on February 1, 1947, Howard and Lucille officially committed to better or worse. They immediately tested that vow by traveling ninety miles north to honeymoon at the Canadian border in International Falls, "The Cold Spot of the Nation." The newlyweds fled the blissful ordeal two days ahead of schedule and returned to the realities of Range living and for Howard—then and forever forth my dad—instant fatherhood.

The author's mother and Gramma B. (Author collection)

Tough Rows to Hoe

DURING THE HARDEST HEART of Range winters, daytime temperatures struggled to rise above zero, often giving up at the minus ten-, twenty-, thirty- and sometimes forty-degree marks. Most mining operations then cut back to skeleton crews that repaired equipment or began pit expansions by clearing timber, removing overburden, and scooping up pockets of soft, loose surface ore. And that iron powder was stockpiled because had it been loaded into railroad cars, it would have frozen into seventy-ton blocks before reaching Lake Superior ports. Not that getting it there would have mattered much, since Great Lakes shipping lanes were also iced shut.

So from the onset of operations in the 1890s, most mines all but closed each winter. And until New Deal public assistance, laid-off miners either found other work or dealt with deprivation. Until the Great Depression, that meant toiling for companies that harvested and milled the vast white pine forests that sprawled north and east. During that era just in Virginia, two sawmills operated at the edges of the city's downtown area. One, the Virginia and Rainy Lake Lumber Company, at its peak was said to be the world's largest such facility, spewing out as many as a million boards a day.

By the time Dad descended into the pits in 1939, however, the timber had been depleted and mills closed. Public assistance had become winter subsistence for many miners. A depressing number cashed their checks at the Range's profusion of bars and liquor stores. Not Dad. Practical and proud, he earned more money than going on "the dole" by working in the heat and grit of Virginia's Staver Foundry. There, he hand-unloaded sand from railroad cars, then used it to set up molds that formed brass fixtures and fittings. Most

The author carrying milk to the separator. (Author collection)

were ordered by mining companies, including the one that had laid him off. Two years later, he was selected for year-round employment by the U.S. Army, which conscripted his services for nearly four World War II years.

In spring 1945, when he mustered out and went back into the mines, he also bought a forty-six-acre farm in partnership with his oldest brother. At $3,100 each, the price was right, and price probably didn't matter, because at heart Dad would rather work the earth than remove it. He could earn more money than public assistance by doing something he loved. And his partnership agreement provided a place to live, on site in a previously vacant farmhouse near aptly named Mud Lake, a shallow, weedy pond a few miles west of Virginia. Two years later, Mom and I joined him.

Our farm, like most of the area's few others, was not a till-the-soil, reap-the-crops operation. The first wave of immigrants who had washed through Minnesota in the 1850s in search of fertile fields deflected away from the Range like water encountering oil. And for good reason. The Mesabi lies within the Canadian Shield, an expansive mass of the earth's oldest, hardest rock. A thick layer of organic matter did once cover the area, but it was scraped away by a series of four massive glaciers that slowly bulldozed through the region. When the last of the mile-thick ice sheets retreated, the only "soil" that remained was, geologically speaking, tissue-thin till atop rocks ranging from pea-size to miles-wide slabs that plunged deep into the earth's crust. The inhospitable terra extra firma coupled with a "reala shorta" growing season meant that the only crops most Range farmers could count on were spring batches of frost-heaved stones and a single summer cutting of hay.

So ours was mostly an Old MacDonald farm, with a barn full of mooing cows, coops of cackling chickens, a pen of snorting pigs, and hives of busy

The author with workhorses Dick and Jim. (Author collection)

bees. Every day, Dad or sometimes Mom set out to Virginia in our tan-and-gold '41 Chev sedan, hauling five-gallon crocks of cream to the Range Cooperative. Every Friday, Dad also delivered eggs to residential customers, and chickens, pork, and honey to restaurants. He returned with the Chev's trunk full of kitchen scraps, which he collected from those accounts plus the city's hospital to feed the hogs.

When heavy winter snows rendered roads risky, Dad hitched his team of workhorses, Dick and Jim, to a large, wood flatbed sleigh to make his deliveries and pick-ups. Along the route, he also sometimes earned extra bucks by pulling stuck cars out of ditches and snow banks. He also hired out to school, service and church groups for winter sleigh and summer hay rides. And he did cultivate one cash crop, an acre of Irish Cobbler potatoes that he sold by the bushel from our back porch.

Our three-bedroom, 1920's, stucco-sided bungalow was heated by a coal-fired boiler that forced steam through cast-iron radiators. The house was electrified, a well supplied water to indoor pipes, and graywater drained out to a small septic field. But the plumbing system lacked a toilet or means to connect

Farmwork. (Author collection)

one. Pre-nuptially, Mom insisted she be spared trips to the outhouse during winter temperatures that could flash-freeze exposed, sensitive body parts. So Dad set a conventional porcelain toilet in a basement corner and inserted a bucket-like liner he had custom-formed from thin sheet metal. Each morning and evening on his way to milk, he removed the receptacle and added its contents to the barnyard pile of animal manure. Mom, Dad, and I bathed in a combination basement sauna/shower. Mom also scrubbed me in a laundry tub. And for clothes and Mom's hair washing, Dad collected naturally soft rainwater in wood-slat barrels placed under house and outbuilding down spouts.

In winter, a couple of the barrels, placed outside our back door, served as a freezer that held freshly slaughtered chickens and pork. We cooked some, but Dad removed most to fill orders phoned in from his Virginia restaurant accounts.

About age three, I began to play at farming. In summer, for instance, I'd spend a few minutes scaling the ridged metal wheels of our Allis Chalmers tractor or pitching a few small rocks onto the potato-field cairn. Then I'd climb aboard our rubber-tired hay wagon for lunch, which Mom packed in a miniature version of the metal pail Dad carried to the mine. That break was immediately followed by quitting time. When I turned four, play segued to work. Dad taught me to ride and drive Dick and Jim. And I helped Dad feed chickens, slop hogs, and milk our ten cows.

Because our electrical service couldn't power a milking machine, we tugged by hand, and I became adept at sending squirts from a teat to a begging barn cat. Dad filled tin pails and lugged them to a separator. Cream went to the co-op, where it was churned into butter. Dad fed the residual skimmed milk to our calves.

During winter layoffs, when farming was Dad's only job, it was cold, tough, and tiring but doable. But when he returned to a full-time, sometimes-overtime schedule in the pits, he stepped onto a fast-moving, round-the-clock treadmill with no off switch. And Dad sometimes grumbled that he received little help from his brother/partner who, "only showed up to collect the checks."

Dad persevered and endured for nearly six years before concluding that, at five feet, five inches tall, he was too short a candle to burn at both ends. In January 1951, he sold his half of the farm to his brother for $3,200, and we relocated a few miles to the Ridgewood Addition to the City of Virginia. Dad's brother and family moved into the farmhouse, and Dad and his former partner rarely spoke to each other again.

Dad spent the next two winter mine layoffs laboring on one of several "track gangs" that maintained and repaired the Range's extensive web of railroad lines. Work was hard, weather often oppressive, but wages above assistance. Then finally, he attained enough seniority at the mine to work there year round. For the next thirty years, he reported for more than 1,500 shifts, including hundreds in below-zero weather. But he returned home wrapped in the warmth of what on the Range passed for stability and security.

March 1, 1946: **Convict cuts me.**

Uncle Sam brought me to a bargain barbershop for my first haircut, which was administered by a woman who had been trained in and just released from prison.

January 16, 1948: **Horse energized car.**

After suffering a thirty-degree-below-zero night, our Chev's battery refused to respond. So, as Dad had to do several times each winter, he hitched workhorse Jim to the car's front bumper, slid onto the driver's seat, engaged the clutch, stuck his head out the window, and ordered Jim to pull. When Jim reached optimum speed, out along Mud Lake Road, Dad pushed the starter, popped the clutch, and revved the engine.

Dad then honked, Jim stopped, and Dad unhitched him. The horse, followed by the Chev, then returned to the barn, where Jim got an extra ration of oats.

January 24, 1948: **Death followed a funeral.**

Against her doctor's advice, Dad's mother, who had chronic high blood pressure, flew to California in an unpressurized plane to attend her brother's funeral. She suffered two strokes after the services and died. Her body was flown home.

March 9, 1948: **Spring tease was temporary.**

Over the past forty-eight hours, the temperature plunged 54 degrees, from +28 to -26.

June 13, 1948: **Kept on a short leash.**

As always before making trips between her ringer washer and clothesline, Mom strapped me into a homemade leather harness and tethered me to a sandbox so I couldn't explore. Like into a nearby abandoned open well.

July 17, 1948: **Could have drowned in rain water.**

I leaned too far over the top of a full, three-foot-high rainwater-collection barrel and silently slipped in headfirst. Mom, watching from the kitchen window, ran out, grabbed my fluttering feet, and extracted me like a plunger out of a syringe. Still clutched in my dripping hand was an orange-flavored sucker, a treat evidently so prized that I would have taken it into the afterlife.

September 15, 1948: **Went skinny selling.**

I watched fascinated each time Mom opened a coffee can with an attached metal key that wound a strip off the top of each container. I saved the keys with the red metal ribbons twisted around them. Then unbeknownst to Mom, I propelled my scooter out onto gravel Mud Lake Road, intending to stop door to far-flung door to offer my collection for a penny each. My sales trip was cut short, however, when my first customer phoned Mom to inform her that not only was I peddling, but nude.

January 21, 1949: **Dad received hush money.**

Following a heavy snowstorm that made rural roads risky for vehicle travel, Dad hitched his workhorses to our large flatbed sleigh to transport eggs and meat to his Queen City customers. Not far from our farm, Dad encountered a stuck car. He recognized the occupants, an unmarried female school teacher and a married prominent businessman. They evidently had set out for our back roads to carry on their secret affair in the man's Chrysler. But in the rush to passion, the man had lost control and imbedded his New Yorker in a snow bank. After workhorses Dick and Jim extricated the vehicle, the man handed Dad a $5 bill and—leaving no doubt to its purpose—directed, "Keep your mouth shut, Howard."

February 11, 1949: **Horsed around town.**

A blizzard had closed most area roads, so Dad once again hitched up Dick and Jim for deliveries. And he invited Mom and me to ride along. After completing his route, Dad set tracks over Virginia's near-deserted main street, parked in front of the Red Owl market, where we bought a few groceries before returning to the farm.

April 1, 1949: **Mom handed me an early one-way bus ticket.**

Mom drove me to the Virginia Greyhound Bus station, bought a ticket to Duluth, and informed the driver that my aunt and uncle would pick me up, not at the bus terminal, but at Garfield Avenue. She then kissed my forehead, and I stepped aboard with my suitcase for the first of many solo trips to—as old-time Finnish Rangers pronounced—"Daloot."

Halfway into the two-hour, sixty-five-mile journey down Highway 53, the bus stopped at Cotton. While the adult passengers drank coffee at the counter inside the Wilbur Cafe, I sat at a table with the driver, who treated me to a small piece of his donut.

We re-boarded and, an hour later, finally broke out of repetitive swamp flatland and dropped 800 feet down a steep hill toward the western tip of the largest Great Lake, Superior.

The author about to make a solo trip to Dulth, 1949. (Author collection)

15

We serpentined past terraced houses along Piedmont Avenue to its end at Garfield, near the city's harbor. Nanna and Uncle Sam stood at the corner. The driver stopped, opened the door, and I stepped into the exotic, mysterious city. Nanna and Uncle Sam indulged me for a week, then drove me back to my Mud Lake farm.

April 30, 1949: **Walter returned.**

Dad, Mom, I, Grandma and Grandpa B, and other family members and friends attended a funeral and graveside ceremony for my genetic father. His remains had been exhumed from a military cemetery in France, flown home and, today, reinterred at a Barfknecht-family plot.

May 17, 1949: **Mom fashioned a brand-new pair of used pants.**

Dad had abused a pair of work pants beyond restoration. So Mom excised frayed sections and other pieces required to downsize to almost my size. She then stitched the usable material back together, with room for me to grow into. Also, the zipper was broken, so Mom replaced it with one from her reserve of notions removed from clothing that had outlived all other usefulness. She then attached suspenders to my loose-fitting trousers, rolled up the cuffs, and hung them from my shoulders.

May 19, 1949: **Was barn baptized.**

The author wearing his brand new used pants. (Author collection)

The amount, texture and velocity of the stuff that plopped and gushed out of our cows' aft orifices fascinated me. So as I sometimes did when one of our Holsteins lifted her tail and let loose, I moved in for a closer look. This time, however, the cow objected to the voyeurism and kicked me into the floor trough that served as her toilet.

June 4, 1949: **Dog departed.**

As usual before helping Dad retrieve cows from the pasture, our farm mutt, Lady, approached me to play. But instead of running, she hopped on three legs, holding her left rear paw up against her side. I asked Dad what was wrong.

"Got kicked by a horse," he replied.

Next day, Lady didn't join me and I didn't see her. I asked Dad where she was.

"Ran away," he replied without looking up.

I suspected not.

Next afternoon, one of Lady's pups, Sport, took over.

June 16, 1949: **Sister didn't survive.**

Mom prematurely gave birth to twins, Carol Jane and Kathy Jean. Virginia's hospital had only one incubator in working condition, however, and it was assigned to Kathy, who was diagnosed most fragile. Carol died two days later, and Dad arranged an unceremonious burial in a family plot. Mom never saw Carol and spent spent seven weeks separated from Kathy, who remained in the hospital until strong enough to come home.

July 18, 1949: **Observed a human feedlot.**

I crossed Mud Lake Road to see if any of the Salo boys wanted to play. I arrived just before their supper time. Mrs. Salo said it wouldn't take long to feed her husband and nine children, all boys, and invited me inside to wait. Shirtless Mr. Salo sat down at a small table. The boys backed up against surrounding walls as Mrs. Salo set down a tub mounded with mashed potatoes and handed Mr. Salo a large spoon. Mr. Salo shoveled spuds into his stubbled face and, when satiated, stabbed the utensil upright into the potato pile and left the room. The boys then surged to the mass like piranhas on a stricken water buffalo.

August 27, 1949: **Got a shocking education.**

Four of the Salo boys plopped me down in front of a fence post. A pair of bare metal wires spaced about three feet apart connected that upright to others around their barnyard. One Salo said, "Touch the bottom wire with this blade of grass." I did.

Another said, "Tap it with this piece of cardboard." I did.

A third handed me a stick and said, "Rub it with this." I did.

The fourth handed me a tin coffee can cover and instructed, "Press this down on it." I did and nothing happened for a second. Then the pulsating current from what I was about to learn was an electric fence sidetracked through the lid, causing my small body to jolt, then tingle.

January 29, 1950: **Survived near-record cold.**

While brewing morning coffee, Mom glanced through our kitchen window at an attached outdoor thermometer and saw that the red alcohol was pooled in the bulb below the lowest, -50° F., mark. She clicked on the radio and heard that last night's temperature had, in fact, bottomed out at -51°.

Dad returned from the unheated barn and reported that the animals were fine. Evidently their bodies generated enough heat that even the water troughs hadn't frozen he said. Dad near-continually fed coal to our furnace boiler for the next twenty-four hours, while the temperature gradually rose to a balmy -10.

April 24, 1950: **Almost suffered from postpartum rage.**

On a cold, damp morning, our sow gave birth to a litter of sixteen, double the normal. Dad hustled the tiny newborns from the birthing pen to our kitchen, where Mom placed them in our oven in a futile attempt to keep the hairless piglets warm and alive. Outside I observed, transfixed and unaware that my knee-high, slip-on rubber boots had sunk deep into the barnyard muck.

During one of his focused round trips, Dad neglected to close the pen gate. The agitated 650-pound sow charged through the opening straight at me. I tried to run, but the quicksand-like ooze suctioned my boots, securing me for a potential filleting by the grimacing animal's bared teeth. Fortunately, Dad was close enough to swoop in, pluck me out of my boots, dash a few steps into the cow barn, and slam shut the split door's bottom half inches from the hog's flat, snot-snorting nose.

June 17, 1950: **Dad suffered a stinging reprisal.**

When a swarm of Dad's honey bees settled in a tree instead of one of his hives, he enveloped himself in beekeeper's protective clothing and relocated their nest. In protest, the bees attacked en masse, weighing down the outfit's normally loose-fitting, netted headgear tight against Dad's neck and face. The form-fit allowed the insects to unleash a fusillade of stings. Dad sprinted to a horse-watering trough and dove in to shed his attackers. Then, still pursued by the swarm, he made a literal beeline for the house.

June 28, 1950: **Joe wasn't Santa.**

I investigated an abandoned one-room schoolhouse near our farm with two older boys, Joe Charmoli and Harvey Hellyer. We climbed a nearby tree, dropped from an overhanging limb onto the pitched roof, and crawled over to the chimney. Joe suggested he could get into the boarded-up building by lowering himself down the brick stack. He climbed in but had only dropped to his armpits when he got stuck. Harvey and I each grabbed an arm and extricated Joe, soot-streaked from his armpits down.

July 20, 1950: **Had a relatively close call.**

I crossed the street from Grandma and Grandpa B's Mt. (Mountain) Iron house to inspect a parked milk truck while the driver made door-to-door deliveries. I crawled underneath. Suddenly, the truck started, and I rolled over onto my belly between the wheels as it backed up.

Grandpa took me to a doctor who administered a lecture and iodine to minor scrapes on my back.

Years later, Mom disclosed that the truck's driver was the father of the soldier who had accidentally shot and killed my father, Walter, in France during World War II.

August 23, 1950: **Dad was flashed.**

Dad pursed his lips and shook his head as he reported that, once again, a neighbor woman had stood nude, silent and motionless in her doorway in full-frontal, clear view of him as he drove our cows from pasture to barn.

September 19, 1950: **Dad didn't detail war wounds.**

I glanced from my floor play spot near Dad's chair as he pulled up his left pant leg and reflexively massaged his shin. The skin was hairless, abnormally white, and mottled.

I asked him why his leg looked that way. "The war. Got grafts," he answered then returned to his newspaper.

So Far Away from Me

As a germinating hayseed, I had flirted enough with the Queen City to look forward to a long-term relationship. While accompanying Dad on his deliveries, I had been fascinated by Virginia's people, homes, and businesses. And I had loved the Saturdays when we added to the throngs of shoppers from surrounding areas that took over the town.

The lines into Virginia had formed practically from the town's founding and promotion by speculators in 1892. The beckoning finger of near-guaranteed employment in area sawmills and iron mines summoned immigrants by the thousands, swelling the settlement into one of the Mesabi's three major population centers. But even as such, by the time of our move, Virginia—at nine square miles and 12,342 residents—was no sprawling, cosmopolitan metropolis. The Queen City was a compact, no-nonsense retailing center wrapped by unpretentious neighborhoods, mine pits, swampland and wilderness.

Chestnut, the main downtown street, ran just six blocks east from a railroad passenger station on the shore of Silver Lake to an abrupt end at a 500-foot-deep, working iron-mine pit. The buildings lining that commercial strip were mostly two-story, conjoined utilitarian boxes constructed of brick as mandated by ordinance after preceding pine tinderboxes had all burned to the ground. Twice. Twenty-seven housed bars and liquor stores, an intoxicating average of four and one-half per block, but down from the seventy-eight such establishments that sotted the street at the peak of the lumbering era.

A variety of sobriety intervened, including hardware stores, pharmacies, grocery stores, "five-and-dimes," department stores, men's and women's clothiers, barbers, beauty shops, seven small cafes, four hotels, three movie theaters, four

20

Virginia, Minnesota, circa 1948.(Virginia Area Historical Society)

full-service gas stations, three new-car dealers, and a homemade candy store. Doctors, dentists, attorneys, and other professionals leased office space in the top four floors of the five-story First National Bank Building, the city's tallest. Individuals and families rented second-story rooms and apartments above many of the other businesses. And just off Chestnut, bench-sitters carried on "heated" topical debates in the men's "Bull Room" at the city's public sauna.

Other businesses spilled back along Chestnut's side streets and lined main arteries that fed into the downtown area. And tucked into neighborhoods were thirty-some small food markets, many of which catered to the more than forty different ethnic groups that had settled the area.

Taxes assessed on the millions of tons of iron ore underlying the area ensured public facilities and services well beyond similar-size cities anywhere. A municipally owned, coal-fired Water & Light plant generated electricity and annually pressured more than a billion pounds of steam to more than 3,000 homes and businesses, making it the largest such heating system in the world.

Downtown (Chestnut Street) Virginia, Minnesota, circa 1948. (Chuck Pottsmith, Virginia Area Historical Society)

A four-story, 125-bed, city-owned hospital dispensed health care from conception to grave, which for many decedents was a short crossing over the street to city-owned Greenwood Cemetery. Summer patients in west-facing rooms could watch golfers play an eighteen-hole, spruce-studded municipal course, which rolled down and out practically from the hospital's foundation. A half mile southeast, a sandy public swimming beach lined 400 yards of the west shore of Silver Lake.

A classic Carnegie-style library shelved 55,000 thousand books plus periodicals, newspapers, vintage sepia-tone stereoscopes, and the latest technicolor 3-D View Master disks. Perhaps because of the long winters with few warm diversions, the Queen City's library at the time boasted the state's highest per-capita book circulation.

But the big-city attraction that I most looked forward to visiting—often—was Olcott Park, forty lushly landscaped, gently sloping, sensory overloaded acres that abutted Greenwood Cemetery. A two-story-tall, shiny steel slide towered over a playground generously outfitted with teeter totters, a jungle gym, balance beams, ring and triangle hand swings, and an assortment of swing sets, sandboxes, and smaller slides. One of the country's first electric fountains—landscaped with stonework and spilling into a three-acre rock garden—spewed multi-colored sprays thirty feet into summer night skies. Also for two hours each summer Sunday evening, a paid forty-piece city band wafted music through the park's elms and spruces from a raised Victorian pavilion. Peacocks, elk, moose, llama, buffalo, white-tail deer, mountain goats, and brown and black bear roamed expansive enclosures behind a greenhouse lush with native and exotic flowers and plants.

But the largest crowds consistently circled "monkey island," a ten-foot tall, eight-foot diameter fieldstone tower perched atop a layered slab-rock pyramid and enclosed by a ten-foot-deep, mostly dry moat. There, Rhesus monkeys were temporarily boarded a dozen or so at a time until being shipped off to research facilities. The playful primates put on near-nonstop daytime performances—scampering in and out of holes in the tower, perching on concrete ledges beneath

Olcott Park's Monkey Island. (Virginia Area Historical Society)

23

the openings, swinging across a swayback rope bridge strung between the skeletons of two long-dead trees, scurrying over the moat's concrete bottom, and treadmill-spinning on an old wood-spoked wagon wheel. Between acts they cocked their heads and contemplated their human onlookers.

They'd get to look at me often, I figured.

Reality, however, didn't match expectations. Not long after Virginia had been officially incorporated and platted in 1895, the booming city burst its boundaries, and small, defined, named "additions" absorbed the overflow. Most near-seamlessly conjoined the core city or other additions.

Ridgewood, the city's southernmost addition, where we moved, however, was stand-alone, nearly cut off, and sometimes left out. Manmade and natural features combined to isolate Ridgewood and confine me to a three-by-four-block activity area. On the south, Ridgewood ended at the beginning of a thicketed lowland mixed with wooded hills that sprawled south fifty mostly uninterrupted miles. A small-plane airfield formed Ridgewood's western border. A rocky ridge upchucked by ancient earth and expanded by mine refuse to support a monstrous iron-ore crushing facility delayed sunrises.

And on the north, an extensive, four-block-wide strip of wasteland separated us from the Queen City itself. Neither mail carriers nor underground pipes from the world's largest steam-heating system cut through the no-man's land. Ridgewooders cut wood or had fuel oil or coal delivered to feed furnaces. And they had to trek through rain, snow, heat, and gloom of night a mile and a half to the post office in town to pick up their mail. Most of Ridgewood lacked paved streets and sidewalks. But we were flush with the city's sewage, which flowed under us to a treatment plant just a half mile south of my front door. From there, pumps discharged effluent into a large, green-slime-covered lagoon hygienically named Three Mile Lake. Though close, the facility stayed pretty much out-of-smell, out-of-mind.

Ridgewood adults and older kids crossed over the lowland on two roads and two sets of railroad tracks that plugged into the action. But for a few more years until I became more independently mobile, the Queen City, though nearer, was not close enough to embrace.

Life Down Under

Necessity plus peer pressure and pride compelled Rangers to make and do as much as possible for themselves.

Dad was no exception, except he was exceptional. He grew, raised or hunted much of our food. He maintained, repaired and rebuilt our cars, appliances, and—well, actually—just about everything material. Sometimes he created what was needed out of salvaged, found, and handcrafted parts. Had one of us kids contracted polio, I was confident Dad could rig an empty fifty-five-gallon oil drum, church-organ bellows, and washer motor into an iron lung.

And he could have done it with one hand—either hand—tied behind his back, because a decade of knuckle-rappings with rulers whipped by school teachers trying to "correct" his congenital left-handedness had left him ambidextrous.

Because of the discomfort dispensed by educators plus family hardship inflicted by the Great Depression, Dad turned his backside to formal education the first day he legally could, when he turned sixteen on February 7, 1935. Using $150 he had earned and saved by trapping and selling wildlife pelts, he purchased forty wooded acres at a tax-foreclosure sale. He spent another three dollars for an inoperative Star auto engine, rebuilt it, then welded a thirty-two-inch, turn-of-the-century, lumbering-era saw blade directly to the flywheel.

His acreage was twelve miles from home, so Dad constructed a one-room log cabin on site where, during lengthy stays, he hunted to supplement packed-in staples. A small wood cookstove doubled as his source of heat. For two years, Dad downed and trimmed popple with an ax then truncated the trunks to ten-foot lengths with his homemade buzz saw. Using a team of horses rented

The author's underground home for two years. (Author collection)

from a nearby farmer for one dollar per day, he skidded the logs to nearby railroad tracks and loaded them onto flatbed cars headed to the local co-op.

Two subsequent years in the Civilian Conservation Corps and U.S. Forest Service, followed by two rookie seasons in the iron mines, three years in World War II foxholes, and six grueling years of simultaneous iron mining and farming further seasoned Dad's self-reliance. So it wasn't surprising that, before our move, Dad determined he would build us a house, as much as possible himself. The decision and process drove us underground for nearly two years.

Dad's first choice for a building site was Virginia's newly created Veteran's Addition. The city's American Legion and VFW posts had platted conjoined land they owned into eighty lots and, in 1949, offered them to area World War II vets via a lottery at $200 each. Dad and three brothers who had also served threw their names into whatever served as the hat. None of the Stoltzes were selected, however.

So Dad paid $500 for a small, vacant parcel in the Ridgewood Addition, a block from his boyhood home where his widower father still lived. In the fall of 1950 Dad contracted out the basement excavation and formation of concrete foundation walls.

Then he took over. He bolted sill plates, strung joists, topped them with pine boards, and waterproofed that flat surface with a double layer of roofing felt. Down inside, he ran wiring and spliced sewer and water pipes. Outside, he hand-shoveled six dump-truck loads of pea rock over drain tiles, then scraped in backfill with our farm tractor. On a thirty-two-degree-below-zero January day, Dad troweled antifreeze-laced cement into a smooth basement floor. And at some point in the process, he constructed an entryway that resembled a conning tower. Combined with the basement's low, black-and-gray profile surrounded by snowdrifts, our new home looked like a submarine surfacing through whitecaps. In late January 1951, our family—including one on the way—went underground.

Finally moved up in the world. (Author collection)

And we were just one crew in a fleet of Virginia subsoilers. Most of the Veteran's Addition lottery winners also sunk basements and lived in them while contractors constructed the upper levels. And other lottery losers dispersed throughout the rest of the city's additions and did same.

Subterranean living was austere but comfortable. Mom hung drapes to partition our contemporary cave into three areas: communal bedroom, living room/kitchen, and bathroom/laundry. A 260-gallon fuel-oil tank, connected to a space heater, dominated our living room from the west wall. (Dad installed the dark-green, metal monolith inside because he preferred #2 fuel oil, which provided more heat for the buck than #1 but coagulated at -32 degrees, a temperature you could count on several times each winter.) The room open-ended on the opposite side into a makeshift kitchen, where cookware, dishes, and supplies were stored in stacked wood crates. A chrome, Formica-topped table doubled as the only counter, and Mom had to move the matching vinyl-cushioned chairs to open the refrigerator or oven door.

With hired help from a retired Swedish-immigrant carpenter, Dad methodically topped our grotto with a compact, 800-square-foot , single-story rectangular box. In December 1952, we moved up in the world. We dispersed from our joint sleeping quarters into three small bedrooms, one for me, one for Mom and Dad, and the third for my sisters. The crates' contents were relocated into locally made birch cabinets. And, to indulge a tic of impractical romanticism on Mom's part, Dad had centered the living room's west wall with a blond-brick fireplace.

Mom then spent months painting walls, staining and varnishing trim, and applying other finishing touches. In late fall 1954, Dad consummated the project by constructing a one-car detached garage.

I played, studied and slept in my pine-paneled bedroom for six years, then gave it up to Kathy and voluntarily descended back to the basement bedroom. By then, Dad had replaced the cloth partitions with pressed-chip board walls, overlaid the concrete floor with linoleum tile, and drywalled the ceilings. I reveled in my private teen haven—complete with the basement bathroom just a few steps away—until leaving my home on the Range five years later.

Kathy left also, but not far, to Minneapolis. Reenie (born 1951) ultimately settled in Reno. Carolyn (born 1954) has moved around also, but only within a few miles from home. Dad lived in the house he built until his death in 2006. And more than sixty years after the groundbreaking, Mom still does.

Cold Passion

W HILE GIVING BIRTH, Range mothers underwent routine episiotomies. Not by doctors, but their offspring, who come into the world wearing ice skates. Well, okay, that painful image is obvious hyperbole. But just about every Range kid does don blades shortly after mastering walking.

My years on our farm, however, delayed my development until almost age six, when we relocated to Ridgewood directly across the street from a natural, outdoor ice rink. Mom and Dad surprised me with a new pair of pre-owned bob skates—double-runner, miniature sleds that were secured to regular winter boots with tiny leather belts. I had no idea I was about to enter into a life-long love affair.

And like another awakening years later, I vividly remember the first time. Outdoor temperature was approaching the day's high of ten below, so Mom layered me in cotton long johns, wool pants, and flannel shirt, all encased by a heavy, brown one-piece snowsuit. She then tugged on an aviator-style, fleece-lined, ear-flapped hat, and wrapped and tied a wool scarf around the snowsuit's upturned collar and over my mouth and nose. I shoved my hands into home-knit wool mittens, then held them out for Mom to pull on leather mitts called "choppers."

Dad cinched on my bobs and gave me an encouraging swat on the butt toward Eighteenth Street. I waddled across and, on hands and knees, scaled the high snowbank that enclosed the rink. At the crest, I stood and looked down at what appeared to be a large pond whose smooth, frozen surface brilliantly mirrored the deep-blue, cloudless sky. I then attempted to step down the bank, but my blades had sunk into the snow, so instead I lurched forward then rolled, arriving at the rink's edge looking like a sugar-coated chocolate pastry. I brushed myself off and cautiously skate-walked across a rough perimeter ring where water had mixed with snow before freezing. When I stepped from the stability onto slick ice, both feet shot out straight forward, dropping

29

me onto my well-padded bottom, with legs out front and hands palms down to each side, like I was sunning on the beach. I next performed a break dance on ice, dropping, flopping and spinning as I struggled to simply stand. When finally upright, I tentatively shuffled my skates while my arms windmilled in a reflexive, gyroscopic attempt to maintain balance. But I fell anyway, perhaps a hundred times before stumbling into the correct technique.

Soon after, I gradually dared stride as fast as my short, skinny legs would propel me. The double blades of each skate scratched parallel arcs on the ice as I effortlessly moved faster than I had ever run. And I was certain that my scarf ends were blowing straight out behind me. The self-created wind chill plus exhilaration brought tears to my eyes as I skated lap after continuous lap. As darkness fell three hours after I had dived into my new adventure, Mom called me in for supper. To recapture the incredible sensation, I returned to the lighted rink that night and devotionally thereafter.

Our Ridgewood rink was one of a dozen spaced throughout our nine-square-mile town, so just about every Queen City resident was no farther than five to six blocks from free, near-unlimited ice time. Most rinks were flooded over summer playgrounds, some of which abutted elementary schools. All were configured generally the same—an expansive oval of public-skating ice conjoined to a hockey rink. Humming mercury lights illuminated the facilities during winter's early darkness.

A three-man city DPW crew maintained the rinks, and their schedule brought them to my ice several times a week. With a small front-end loader, one man removed fallen snow from the ice and piled it around the rink's edges. (By midseason, the banks were high enough for us to plummet down their steep sides on sleds, cardboard, or just our snowsuit-covered behinds and shoot out onto the ice.) A second worker scoured the surface with a small tractor fronted by a spinning bristled brush that sent up clouds of snow dust. Meanwhile, a close-to-retirement man afflicted with a neurological condition causing his head to rhythmically bob up and down as though continuously nodding "yes" connected a four-inch canvas hose to a hydrant, then expertly sprayed water to create a smooth, frozen surface.

Skaters at all rinks changed from boots to blades plus came out of the cold as needed in small warming facilities, each loosely supervised by a paid attendant. Inside our crude, claustrophobic, windowless wood hut, plank benches crowded a central pot-belly stove, fed with coal by someone we knew only as the "shack guy." The cast-iron heater's top also served as a dryer for wet mittens, and the stench from overcooked wool often permeated the close quarters.

And at least once a season, the over-stoked stove's thin, metal flue, which poked uninsulated through the roof, would ignite the abutting wood boards. At the shack guy's, "Ah shit!" alarm, those of us inside methodically evacuated ourselves plus as many boots and mittens as we could grab and carry, while the shack guy furiously threw shovelfuls of snow up at the flames. Usually he succeeded, and the smolders hissed and steamed out. But on occasion, bona fide firefighters had to douse flickers. Next day a city worker would tack a layer of tin over the damage, and the following summer the metal patch would be replaced with new boards, which then dried to fuel the following winter's fire. But the shack never burned down, and no kid, boot, or mitten was ever injured.

For my first couple of seasons, I mostly skated solo or scooted around with other neighborhood kids on the public area. We often played pom-pom-pullaway. A single skater who had volunteered to be "it" stood at the center of the large rink. The rest of us lined up at one edge and en masse attempted to skate across to the other side without being tagged by "it." Those tagged also became "its" for the next run, and the crossings continued until everyone had been caught.

We also cracked the whip. The rink's size accommodated a hand-in-hand line of as many as a dozen whippersnappers, who would accelerate to a speed at which the kid at the tip would be centrifugally forced out of his or her mitts to a surrounding snowbank impalement.

We gathered at the rink regardless of conditions. When snow blanketed the ice between scheduled cleanings, we pushed shovels in front of us, clearing a labyrinth of skating lanes. On days windy enough to stall forward progress, we turned our backs, put hands on hips to form our parkas into mini-sails, and blew across the nature-cleaned ice without having to take a stride. And we didn't confine ice time to the warming-shack schedule—weekdays from 4:00 to 9:00 p.m. and weekends from noon until nine. We hit the ice early weekend mornings and, when old enough, skated weeknights after lights-out until our parents commanded us home. When the shack wasn't open, we laced up our skates at home and walked to and from the rink, which didn't dull our blades, because snow sometimes compacted so hard on sidewalks and roads, we could actually skate on them.

When spring daytime temperatures warmed enough to begin melting the ice, we'd get up early on weekends after night-time refreezes and skate on thick, frozen areas that lingered. Initially, we skip-strided over narrow dirt strips that interrupted large patches of ice. Then, as the gaps grew wider and the ice surfaces smaller, we performed Evel Knievel-style jumps. And when we missed, our skates jammed into the soft muck, and we pitched forward and down to reluctantly kiss the ice goodbye until next season.

January 31, 1951: **Just your average January.**

Average temperature for the month was -5° F. Average low was -15°. Average high, +5°.

February 1, 1951: **Started milk runs.**

While living on our farm, we had plenty of milk to drink, direct from our cows. Now that we lived in town, we made the first of what would be years of regular trips to our former neighbors the Hellyers for our supply. Dad and I entered their milk house, grabbed eight glass quarts from the cooler, and plunked them into our new, homemade wood carrier. Dad tossed four quarters into a dented metal bowl that held coins and bills. He removed four pennies change, and we headed home without seeing any of the Hellyers.

February 28, 1951: **Naturally in the dark.**

"Gary, get up. It's time for school," Mom hollered.

"Can't be," I yelled back. "It's pitch black."

Mom snapped on our bedroom light and, while tossing clothes onto my bed, explained that a snowstorm during the night had buried our low-profile domicile, blotting out all daylight. As I dressed, Dad shoveled out our window areas to restore natural illumination.

June 4, 1951: **Second sibling added.**

Mom gave birth, without complications, to Laurene (Reenie) Jeanette.

July 1, 1951: **Plane crashed nearby.**

I heard on radio station WHLB that, during a mid-morning takeoff from Virginia's small airport, two blocks west of our house, a small plane had nose-dived seventy-five feet, bounced off the LaVigne family's lawn, and crashed into their house's foundation.

I walked the six blocks to the site. The damage to plane and house didn't seem to be extensive, but an excited classmate who lived nearby told me that he had seen, "a guy crawling around with a big hole in his head." The pilot and all three passengers had in fact suffered head lacerations, and one had crawled around in a daze until help quickly arrived. But none of the four suffered life-threatening injuries. Mrs. LaVigne had seen the troubled incoming plane in time to grab her two-year-old son and dash out the back door.

A year later, the airport was relocated south to an unpopulated, swamp-surrounded area where, in 2002, Minnesota U.S. Senator Paul Wellstone, family members, and entourage would die in a crash.

July 17, 1951: **Dad nabbed a roof runner.**

Our and other flat-topped, below-ground living quarters also served as hard-to-resist outlets for pre-teen mischief. After dark, when inspired or conspired, individuals or small groups would sneak up to a targeted basement, jump the two feet from ground to roof, and sprint across. Down inside, the exercise sounded like a thundering herd of horses. Of more practical significance, the hit-and-runners could tear the fragile tarpaper protection against leaks. So at the startling first footfall, Dad would leap from his chair and double-step up and out the entry tower in pursuit of the raiders.

Tonight he actually got one, a slow-footed, slow-witted neighbor who crouched, giggling behind a bush in the vacant lot next door. Dad grabbed the eleven-year-old's shirt collar with one hand and the kid's leather belt on his butt side with the other, then delivered him—dangling with a Wrangler wedgy—to his parents a block away. Next day, the perpetrator returned with a bucket of tar and brush in hand and performed a two-hour, hands-and-knees inspection and repair of the roof.

September 10, 1951: **Reading was for the birds.**

Miss Keto divided our first-grade class into three groups based on her evaluation of reading potential. I was sure I would be placed in the top group, Bluebirds, who would get to have fun with Dick and Jane at the fastest pace. So I was devastated when she assigned me to the second-tier Robins, who would read fewer books. But at least I ranked above the Cardinals, who would be lucky to make it through one book during the school year.

Two days later, Miss Keto elevated me to the Bluebirds, and I flew through the Scott Foresman series.

October 31, 1951: **Weather no treat.**

I went out on my first-ever Halloween trick-or-treating rounds. In fourteen-degree temperatures.

Log-ged Determination

To put a roof over his family's head, Uncle Lee raised the Range resourcefulness bar to a remarkable high by sinking to a new low.

In the years following World War II, Uncle Lee, Dad, and other Range veterans built rather than bought homes for their families. Necessity and culture compelled many to carry out much of the construction themselves, over time as finances allowed. Most purchased materials at local lumber yards. Some got by cheaper by picking through rough-sawn piles at backwoods sawmills. And a few brought down expenses even further by downing trees at their building sites and hauling them to commercial mills to be cut and planed.

And then there was Lee Marconett, a three-year Navy vet and Range lifer who married the oldest of Dad's two younger sisters, Phyllis. While indulging a lumbering-era old-timer's reminisces, he learned of a hidden treasure-trove of prime building material—hundreds, maybe thousands of white-pine logs, cut into sixteen-foot lengths and free for the taking. Complication was, the cache lay scattered across the bottom of Hibbing Bay, one of hundreds of indentations that form Lake Vermilion's 1,200 miles of convoluted shoreline. During turn-of-the-twentieth-century winter cutting seasons, loggers had covered the thousand-acre cove's thick ice with sixteen-foot-high stacks of timber. After spring thaw, "drivers" floated the logs to nearby sawmills. Before the move, however, the enormous weight of the huge piles sank them into the twelve- to fifteen-foot deep water, jamming some of the lowest logs into crevices between the rocks and boulders that formed the lake bottom. The submerged, trapped timbers were ignored and abandoned.

That is until Uncle Lee decided to retrieve the drowned wood and give it a new home. For three years beginning in 1950, he fished for the pine. Since sport anglers crowded the popular bay on summer days, Uncle Lee limited his specialty seasons to spring and fall. Whenever possible then, he drove his 1949 Chevrolet flatbed truck up US-53 thirty miles from his West Virginia home to Hibbing Bay where, conveniently, his uncle owned a cabin. There, he launched his eighteen-foot wood boat and, propelled by a five-horse-power Evinrude outboard, trolled for timber. Spring ice-out action usually thrust up a few logs so that their ends—branded with a "TLC" (Tower Lumber Company) logmark—poked out of the water. Uncle Lee simply roped and pulled them out and to shore. But most of the pine remained lodged and hidden beneath the cloudy water.

To retrieve those submerged, large pickup sticks, Uncle Lee custom-crafted a pike pole. After sharpening one end of a large, flat file, he heated the metal soft, twisted it a few turns, then welded it to the end of a sixteen-foot section of three-quarter-inch steel pipe. From his boat, he plopped the pole's pointed tip into the water and gripped the above-board end in his right hand while controlling the Evinrude's throttle and tiller with his left. Slowly crisscrossing the bay, he sensed his pine-finder scrape over rocks to a satisfying thunk on wood. While maintaining contact with the log, Uncle Lee then maneuvered to bring the pole close to vertical, whereupon he harpooned the Moby Stick.

He then raised his quarry to the surface and towed it to shore. Even at the slow speeds generated by the straining mini-outboard, the wake washed off the wrinkled, gray bark that still wrapped most logs to reveal beautiful, smooth, alabaster columns. Most of the timbers measured eight to ten inches in diameter and sixteen feet in length. And, given that the company that felled them had folded in 1910, all had been perfectly preserved in the cold fountain of youth for at least forty years.

On shore, Uncle Lee geared up his truck's power takeoff, fastened to a winch and cable that dragged the logs out of the water and onto the truck bed. He then delivered his loads a couple of miles to Ryan's Sawmill, near Cook. Workers there preferred to cut his logs immediately, claiming that the water-soaked, clear pine was kinder and gentler to their three-foot-diameter blades than pitch-filled, knotted specimens out of the forest. Ryan's milled the pine into dimensional lumber, then racked it to dry.

Uncle Lee's part in the not-so-mass production was labor-intensive, repetitive, and inherently low-output. During a typical session after work stoking boilers at the DW&P railroad's roundhouse, he fished out four or five logs, each of which yielded three or four pieces of lumber. He quadrupled that output on days off from work. But still, his first season's harvest yielded only enough two-by-fours to frame a two-car garage next to the small, old house he and Aunt Phyl had purchased and lived in for four years.

They stored their furniture in the new outbuilding and, with their two young children, temporarily moved into the house where Uncle Lee was born, with his parents a half block down the street. During the next few months, Uncle Lee tore down their old house and started a new-build on an expanded foundation.

For two more years, Uncle Lee made round trips to Hibbing Bay until Ryan's had milled enough material to frame his dwelling. Ryan's also culled knotted logs and milled them into bevel-edged paneling, which by the end of the three-year operation, covered only the walls of one small bedroom.

After sheathing and roofing their unassuming ranch-style home, Uncle Lee and family moved in. Methodically, Uncle Lee replaced privacy sheets and bed-spreads tacked to the interior two-by-fours with drywall, and otherwise almost finished his ongoing project. More than sixty years after lancing his first log, he still lives in his homemade home. Aunt Phyl—terminally ill in 2011—chose to die there.

Uncle Lee does have one regret about his unmatched undertaking. He was sure he would fill his tackle box with lures that anglers had snagged into the logs and snapped off. But he retrieved only a single, common Dardevle.

January 7, 1952: **Didn't know wolves were near my door.**

"Did you see the the wolves strung up outside the airport last week?" classmate Dave Glumack asked me on our way into school after the holidays.

"No. From where?" I quizzed, knowing none roamed our immediate area.

Dave said he had seen the carcasses strapped to the skis of small planes that had skimmed his house on their landing paths. So he walked over to check and, while watching men temporarily hang the wolves' remains from the hangar wall, learned that they were bounty hunters who had shot the animals near Ely.

"What's a bounty?" I asked.

"Somebody pays them $35 for each wolf," Dave answered.

January 12, 1952: **Grandpa B. was reluctant to reveal.**

After returning home from a longer session than usual at the American Legion bar, Grandpa hoisted me onto his lap. He then briefly reminisced about his World War I army service, recalling that he had inadvertently averted combat because he had a talent for braiding hemp into rope. As a result, he spent his two-year drafted hitch in Mississippi fashioning harnesses and other gear for mules and horses.

Grandpa's oldest son, my father, had been killed in World War II and his youngest son recently wounded in Korea, but I had never heard him speak about war before and wouldn't again.

February 7, 1952: **Dad was blind-sided.**

Mom hung up the phone, turned to me and said, "Dad's been hurt. They say he's okay. Art's bringing him home."

Twenty minutes later, I heard our entryway door open and saw Art Lambert, Dad's long-time co-worker and friend, steadying my steadfast father. Thick gauze patches had been taped over Dad's eyes, and his face was blotched and swollen. Art helped Dad down the stairs into our basement living quarters, and Mom then took his arm and guided him to his chair.

Turned out, a malfunctioning road grader Dad was operating had caused him to check the coolant level. Unbeknownst to him and for reasons unknown, someone had removed antifreeze and replaced it with water. So, though Dad had carefully loosened the radiator cap, steam had exploded against his face.

I stared. Dad couldn't. He didn't say much but seemed to be more mad than in pain. Next morning, Mom removed his eye pads just before Art picked him up for work.

March 16, 1952: **She may have lost _her_ marbles.**

I mentioned to my Sunday school teacher that, for my birthday, Grandma and Grandpa B had given me ten marbles. The severe, thirty-something woman ripped off her wire-rimmed glasses, emphasizing eyes bulging with righteousness, then hissed, "If you play marbles, you'll go to Hell! It's a sssssin! It's GAMBLING!"

Puzzled more than frightened, I reported the exchange to Mom and Dad, who just shook their heads. So, God's spokeswoman be damned, I set a goal: play long and well enough to fill a large, old, dented metal wash basin with 1,000 marbles.

I never entered the annual, spring, city-wide tournament, because grade winners from prelims at each elementary school competed for only trophies and front-page newspaper photos, not marbles. Instead, during snow-free months, I near-exclusively played a high-stakes, unsanctioned street game called "pot."

In late spring 1954, I dropped the thousandth marble into the pan, then shoved it and its contents into forgotten darkness behind and under our bottom-most basement stair. On a Sunday morning just before church.

March 20, 1952: **Civil War cancelled.**

Our morning and afternoon outdoor recesses were unsupervised, so we improvised. This afternoon, several dozen boys from grades one through six—me included, and many wearing replica Civil War caps—mustered into Yank and Reb armies on opposite sides of the skating rink that abutted our school. Noncombatants congregated on the surrounding snowbanks.

They witnessed an epic battle as we pelted each other with snowballs, some centered by ice chunks, a few with rocks. Each side advanced into close-quarters action, and our battlefield became spotted red from bloody noses and superficial scalp wounds. I returned to my classroom undamaged. But our school nurse treated so many casualties that our principal banned future such combat.

But we were still allowed to rough and tumble at our standard free-for-all, "King of the Hill."

April 12, 1952: **Twice botched my bread.**

I had ingested my parent's admonitions that food should never be wasted. But I had not completely digested, I discovered when I burned the first slice of bread I had ever toasted myself. As I pinched the hot, charred piece toward the garbage can, Mom snatched it, scraped the black off into the can, spread jam over the remaining nooks and crannies, and handed the slice back to me.

May 22, 1952: **Pasta, please.**

"You get to eat all the ice cream you want," is, of course, what I was promised before I was wheeled down a hospital corridor to have my tonsils and adenoids removed. A nurse then placed what looked like a small metal kitchen strainer over my nose and mouth, covered it with a cloth, and poured a strong-smelling liquid called ether on it. Seconds later, I woke up with a sore throat.

Next morning, Mom picked me up, and on the way home I threw up. But not long after arriving, I did request and eat—hot, soothing macaroni.

June 30, 1952: **Dad dove back in time.**

As a storm passed through during the night, an exceptionally loud thunderclap woke me. I then heard Mom talking to Dad. I couldn't hear the words, but her voice was forceful, calm and reassuring. In the morning I asked her about the unusual episode. Dad had been startled awake by the boom, she explained, and had reflexively scrambled to a foxhole no longer there or needed.

July 15, 1952: **Camp construction nearly cost a thumb.**

In a vacant, brush-filled lot next to our basement home, I selected a pair of saplings about five feet apart and, with my pocket knife, set out to trim out forks in each about four feet above ground. I then planned to support a horizontal stick across the crotches and lean a wall of branches and brush against that crossmember. I prepared the first upright without incident. I then grabbed the second with my left hand and pushed hard with my knife-held right to remove an extraneous shoot. The growth sheared off so unexpectedly fast and easy that my freshly sharpened steel blade also sliced and slammed nearly to bone halfway between the knuckles of my left thumb.

For a stunned, slow-motion second, I examined a _Gray's Anatomy_ layered look at a real body part—mine. Then as pain rushed and blood gushed, I pinched the gaping wound with my shirt bottom and ran inside our house. There, Mom calmly doused the gash with Mecurochrome and embalmed my thumb with Johnson & Johnson gauze and white tape.

I returned and finished my lean-to, then read comic books in my private domain. That night, someone—presumably one of the older neighborhood kids who destroyed for pleasure—scattered my shelter back to nature.

Combustible Candy

August 1, 1952

I HAD HEEDED MY PARENTS' WARNINGS, "Don't play with matches." And Smokey the Bear classroom posters and Roy Rogers radio announcements had reinforced their message. But neither Smokey nor Roy nor Mom and Dad had advised that I shouldn't watch others play with matches.

On a windy morning, classmate Ricky Semon and I met up at the playground across our separate streets. There in summers, timothy grass, clover and weeds replaced our winter skating rink. A hot, dry week ago, a city worker had mowed the thick vegetation.

I shuffled toward Ricky, who intently hunched over something inside a sand box that abutted our cold-weather warmup shack. His pose resembled *Weekly Reader* illustrations of prehistoric humans crouched, mesmerized by their discovery of fire. The image came to life when I reached Ricky. He pinched a book of paper matches in his left hand and, one by one, plucked them out with his right, conscientiously closed the cover before striking, then flipped the flickering slivers into the sand. Exhilarated, frightened and silent, I anticipated watching Ricky similarly dispatch the remaining matches. But instead, he tested the incendiary properties of newspaper, cloth, cardboard, and other debris the wind had swept into and around the sandbox.

His burning experimentals followed matches into the sand until he ignited a Hershey Bar wrapper. Residual chocolate melted and stuck the paper to his fingers, and he reflexively bolted upright while flapping his hand to loose the mini-torch. He succeeded, and the wind carried it a couple of yards, where flame-framed, "HEY," lit into the tinder-dry clippings.

We tried to stomp out the burning patch, but the wind whipped the flames into a fast-moving, foot-high wall of fire that within minutes charred the field, sending field mice scurrying across the streets. Fortunately, the playground's boundary roads also acted as fire lanes that contained the blaze. And the wind's direction swept the burn away from the wood shack.

A neighbor had observed the misadventure and called the fire department. But by the time a small, self-contained pumper arrived, the blaze had burned out. As a few final wisps of smoke curled up, a policeman also pulled up in a squad car. Ricky had fled with the mice and hid his skinny self behind a thick-girthed spruce in his yard. I, on the other hand, during the dawn of a life-long compulsion to not miss out on anything, observed as I sauntered to the front of our basement home. A lone fireman and the officer both lit up and smoked cigarettes, then flipped the smoldering butts onto the blackened field. I wondered what Smokey would say.

As they slid back into their vehicles and pulled away from the scorched earth, I plopped onto our barren dirt yard, blithely unaware that, though I had not struck a match, I was an accomplice. The cop stopped to talk with the reporting neighbor, who pointed to us perpetrators. The squad car turned down my street, and I was overcome with the feeling I had experienced a couple of years before, when Mom had lifted my dinner plate, revealing the to-me inedible bread crusts I had "hidden" under its edges. I removed my stub-brimmed cap, hid it behind my behind, and busted dirt clods. I figured the disguise from the cap-doffing plus the casual play would confuse the cop. He'd judge that this innocent-looking little chucker couldn't possibly have been the one involved.

The ruse didn't work. The squad car eased over to the wrong-way side of the street and stopped directly in front of me. The driver's door slowly opened seemingly by itself, and a Humpty Dumpty-shaped man inside motioned me to him. I complied and approached his large, dark armpit soakings. He grunted a gruff, nicotine-breath reprimand while ratcheting a pair of handcuffs open and closed. He warned that should I ever be involved in such delinquency again, he would squeeze the shackles so tightly around my wrists their bite would dent my skin. Then, pointing toward two poles sometimes joined by a volleyball net, he threatened that, after the cuffing, he would tie me in a gunny sack and hang me there for a day.

And finally, he counseled me to tell my parents what had happened before he did. He shut his car's door, shouted out the open window that he would be talking with Dad soon, then moved on to Ricky.

41

Mom was busy down inside our basement home and obviously hadn't seen either the incident or interrogation or she would have been out volunteering to personally place me in the gunny sack. And Dad was at work. So I took a chance and said nothing. That is until I was sure the folks' statute of limitations had run out—some fifty years later.

August 11, 1952: **Bought cigarettes.**

As he sometimes did, after supper Dad handed me a quarter and directed me to walk the block across the playground to Ridgewood Grocery and buy him a pack of Lucky Strikes. The Pietrini family operated the small store out of a front downstairs room of their two-story house. Mr. Pietrini handed me the Luckies as I plinked the quarter onto the glass countertop.

We never again made the exchange. Dad, who had started with war-rationed smokes, soon quit cold turkey.

Ridgewood Grocery remained a neighborhood convenience for another five years, until the rhythmically expanding Pietrini family converted the store into needed living area.

August 23, 1952: **Rolled Grandpa's car.**

Grandpa B parked in front of a market on Mountain Avenue, near his Mt. Iron home. He then handed me two quarters to buy comic books there, while he visited Mac's Bar, a few doors down. I returned first, plopped down on the front seat of Grandpa's black 1949 Mercury, and flipped through my five purchases.

I interrupted the comics to fiddle with the levers that interrupted the Merc's metal dashboard. Then I squirmed down to examine the area around the foot pedals. I spotted what looked like a small, inverted metal cup set into the floorboard above and to the right of the gas pedal. Curious, I pushed on it with both hands. The car groaned and, angle-parked, lurched to a curb stop.

When Grandpa returned, I hid behind my literature so that I didn't make guilty contact with his good eye. (A mining accident had blinded the other.) I did peek, however, to watch him push in the clutch with his left foot and depress the device—the starter—with his right.

October 12, 1952: **Early writing effort rejected.**

On my own at home, I spent most of the day creating a scroll "newspaper" as I imagined it would have appeared during Columbus's time. I hand-wrote an account of his discovery of the New World, with quotes from captain and crew plus sidebar stories, such as how Queen Isabella reacted and what commoners thought.

I rolled it up and next day proudly presented the extracurricular effort to my teacher, Miss Oyen. She said, "I don't think anyone but you would be interested in this, Gary," and placed it in her desk drawer without unfurling it.

October 20, 1952: **Dad explained the fundamentals of politics.**

A couple of sixth graders came to school wearing circular, metal "I Like Ike" buttons. They also handed out extras, so I pinned one on.

At home, Dad snatched off Ike's likeness, threw it in the garbage, and imparted, "Republicans are for rich people. Democrats are for the working man."

Dwight D. Eisenhower became president but—like Republicans before and after—with few votes from Rangers.

November 8, 1952: **Introductory bar visit was sobering.**

Grandpa B escorted me into Mac's Bar for the first time. I figured he wanted me to see the Range-renowned display of heads and complete mounted specimens of what looked to be every animal—including several albino versions—that roamed northern Minnesota. I stood transfixed by the lifelike dead partridge, duck, porcupine, bobcat, rabbit, squirrel, otter, mink, weasel, muskrat, wolf, eagle, owl, and fox.

My spell was broken when Grandpa placed his hands on my shoulders, gently turned me to face the men at the bar, and with sorrow and pride said, "This is Walter's son."

As the men nodded solemnly, I began to understand how special I was.

Hockey Practices

OUR HOCKEY RINK WAS MAGNETIC, pulling the steel skate blades of just about every neighborhood boy onto its surface. The attraction was powerful and fundamental. Hockey was a basic blast—an unsupervised, free-spirited, stick-swinging, puck-slapping explosion of speed, spitting and swearing. And that was just on the way to the rink.

Once there, it got even better. We skated faster than we could run and manipulated a hard rubber disk with a wood stick, while crashing into each other inside a small, slick space confined by boards. Plus, during the long winters, there were few other outlets

The author and his dad at the hockey rink across from their house. (Author collection)

for boyhood energy. So any time I could, I played the greatest game going.

Adults rarely supervised or organized us, but we weren't disorganized. At the start of a session, we split up the two best players, who then alternately chose team members from the available pool. As players left or arrived, we reorganized to equalize. Consensus came easy, because we played together so often, we all knew where everyone fit. Girls were not discouraged from participating, but only one—Gracie Tekautz, the youngest of eleven children—took the ice with us. And she was always an early pick.

No matter how many players, no matter their talent, everyone played. At once. If twenty kids showed up, the on-ice lineup would be ten per side. Cold com-

44

manded the egalitarianism. No way would anyone stand or make anyone else stand frigid, waiting to substitute. In our small, isolated neighborhood, however, we usually played with a near-regulation five to seven players per side. During double-digit, below-zero temperatures, we sometimes skated with only two or three hardy or foolhardy diehards per team. During blizzards, when the rink was vacant, I sometimes, with only driving snow as my opponent, performed solo.

Our group competitions followed few official rules. No one possessed protective equipment, so out of mutual respect and self-preservation, we didn't deliberately body check or raise the puck off the ice to pass or shoot. Also, "Keep sticks on the ice" was mantra. And since neither blue lines nor center red lines marked our rink, icing and offsides never interrupted the flow.

Our rink measured about three-fourths regulation size. So we were sometimes literally hit with hockey's #1 survival axiom—keep your head up. Though body checking wasn't allowed, if we skated looking down at the ice, we'd likely end up seeing stars after accidentally crashing into another head-downer. The small rink also demanded development of stick-handling and passing skills. And the uninterrupted play forced superb conditioning.

We grade-school kids hit the hockey ice weekend mornings (while teenagers slept in), Friday and Saturday nights (when most older boys were socializing), and sometimes weekdays after school. Junior- and senior-high-school boys and, occasionally, adults occupied the ice other times. After rink lights-out, puckers of all ages fired wrist-shot raisers against the boards, sending fusillades of rifle-like cracks echoing through the neighborhood.

When the big boys took over the hockey rink and few skaters were on the public area, the shack guy let us kids use our sticks and pucks there. Sometimes we set up snow-chunk goals and tried to play actual hockey. But the absence of boards resulted in annoying retrievals of errant pucks. So, more often we played "keep away." One kid "ragged" the puck and everyone else tried to take it away, whereupon whoever did became the next puck handler and so on until we quit from exhaustion. When by myself with stick and puck on the big rink, I'd set up a snow-chunk obstacle course, then skate and stickhandle through it.

We also played in the streets, running on rubber boots while passing and shooting a puck-size slice of a solid rubber ball. Using our sticks like Ginsu knives, we carved and carried four cubes of compacted snow from roadside banks and set them as goals about 100 feet apart. Rink rules applied, but we lifted the ban on raisers. Cement curbs topped with plow-produced snowbanks mostly kept the slice in play except for shots on goal.

When cars drove through our street rink, we moved to the sides, waved, and pointed to our snow goals. Most drivers steered clear, but an occasional senior who didn't navigate well would crush one or more. We still smiled and waved because, well, they were somebody's grandparent, and it didn't take long to Samurai out replacements.

Also in the street, I shot ice or snow chunks at a nearby utility pole while waiting for the school bus at my corner stop. When it arrived, I lanced my stick into the snow, then plucked it out after school. A rink abutted my James Madison elementary, but skates, sticks, and pucks were prohibited during school hours. So, during recess we played soccer on ice, using our feet to pass and shoot anything available roughly puck size—ice chunks, lumps of coal, even an occasional frozen dog turd. Inside, we played desktop hockey, "stick handling" and shooting tiny paper wads with wood pencils into our empty, obsolete inkwells or, with the teacher's back turned, snapping a paper puck to a kid across the aisle who would deflect the pass into his inkwell.

We lived hockey, only vaguely aware as kids that our devotions had been and were practiced throughout the Range. And still are. For more than nine decades at hundreds of Mesabi rinks, tens of thousands of kids have played an incalculable number of hours of hockey.

So much metaphoric raw milk in such a small container has continually floated a thick layer of cream out into hockey's highest echelons. The number of Rangers who have played college, olympic and professional hockey rivals that of any comparable Canadian area. A few of my favorite close-to-homers:

- Three players on the "Do you believe in miracles" gold-medal-winning 1980 U.S. Olympic team were hockey-raised on the Range: John Harrington, Virginia; Buzz Schneider, Babbitt; and Mark Pavelich, Eveleth. Pavelich went on to a career with the New York Rangers, where he set a rookie team-scoring record.
- Eveleth's Johnny Mayasich, rated by many as the greatest U.S. amateur ever, was key to the 1960 U.S. Olympic team winning the country's first gold medal in hockey.
- The three Carlson brothers. The real-life inspiration for the "Hansen" brothers (and two of whom played the Hansens) in the classic movie *Slapshot* grew up one block from my Ridgewood home.
- Sam Lopresti, Frank Brimsek, and Mike Karakas, three Eveleth na-

tives responsible for the small community being labeled "Goalie Town USA." Lopresti, while playing for the NHL's Chicago Black Hawks on March 4, 1941, set an NHL record for most saves in a game by a goaltender (83) that still stands. Brimsek recorded ten shutouts in his first NHL season, with the Boston Bruins in 1938-1939, earning him the nickname "Mr. Zero" and the NHL Rookie of the Year award. He also helped the Bruins win the Stanley Cup in his first year and again in 1940-1941. Karakas, the NHL's first American-born goaltender, played six seasons for the Chicago Black Hawks.

Though unable to rise anywhere near their levels, I became proficient enough to skate to a lifetime's worth of fun. When I didn't make our high school's varsity team, I resumed play at my Ridgewood rink, then intramural competition at the University of Minnesota, followed by organized or pick-up hockey wherever I was. Anytime I could, I played the greatest game going.

When I turned fifty, I joined a team in a league that required that age as the entry level for players. Not only was I a rookie again but also considered to be part of my team's youth movement. Seriously. Our goaltender turned seventy that year.

He strapped on the pads three more seasons, playing up to his career-ending buzzer with a man's passion and a little-boy's joy.

The author (seond from the right, front) after his final season. (Author collection)

Frozen Solutions

THE BRUTALITY OF MESABI WINTERS is the stuff of fearful legend. For good reason. Minnesota's coldest-ever temperature—*sixty degrees below zero* actual, no wind-chill factor—numbed Tower, sixteen miles northeast of Virginia, on February 2, 1996. The previous record-low bottomed out at minus fifty-nine near the Range's southwest tip ninety-seven years before. In the winters and area between, nature took sporadic shots at the record by plunging thermometer alcohol below the minus fifty mark. A few times each season, guaranteed, temperatures approached forty below. Minus twenties were too common to command conversation. And January average temperatures had no higher aspiration than to flirt with zero.

To most outsiders, the concept of enduring such cold is incomprehensible. But we were born into it. It was our reality. Not only did we not complain, we took pride in our hardiness. And it turns out we did, in fact, physiologically acclimatize. When scientists finally warmed up to cold research, they discovered that people like us, subjected to frigid temperatures over time, did develop increased tolerance. We metabolically generated more heat, more efficiently than outsiders.

Yup, but we kids were dumb, careless, and oblivious enough to test the limits, sometimes with painful results. Most of the time we cocooned ourselves in layers of clothing, including covering our ears with hat flaps or wool toques, double-layered with a parka hood. But beginning in late elementary grades, in a contagious macho display, we boys removed all headwear when out of parents' sight. To mitigate heat loss through our especially vulnerable ears while appearing figuratively cool, we would thrust up a shoulder and bend an ear down to meet it, alternating from side to side, like a stop-action Stevie Wonder sway. Then when we felt stinging bites by ice crystals forming in cellular fluid, we'd remove mitts and cup our ears. The techniques, however, only delayed the inevitable—ears frozen numb and white. Each subsequent exposure froze them progressively faster. And with each freeze-thaw cycle, our ears thickened while slowly swiveling forward perpendicular to our skulls. The unique configuration made us appear capable of flight.

Feet most often went numb while playing hockey. To avoid flopping around the rink, we laced our skates so tight that we cut off circulation, and our feet froze fast. Since they also lost feeling, we usually didn't notice until after our sessions.

Unlacing then unleashed excruciating pain. Warm, red blood surging into our cadaver-white feet inflicted the sensation of thousands of tiny needles rapidly and repeatedly stabbing the soft, sensitive skin. Also, our thin-leather skate boots didn't much mitigate random whacks from sticks and pucks. But again we didn't feel the effects until the afterglow, which added the agony of being rhythmically pounded with ball-peen hammers.

We tried alleviating the pain with longstanding folk remedies, all of which unknowingly added to our misery and, according to later research, risked causing tissue damage. We rubbed our feet with snow. We held them inches from the shack's stove. At home we immersed them in hot water and massaged them. But in spite of our misguided mistreatment, no one ever had even a little toe amputated.

Fingers rarely froze, because we could artificially warm them naturally. At the first hint of discomfort, we removed mittens and squeezed our hands under our armpits or between our thighs. Or we blew warm breath on them while friction-generating heat by rubbing them together. We then tucked our digits back into loose-fitting, insulating mittens, which allowed unrestricted, warming blood circulation.

Wrists, however, did occasionally freeze, with the strangest effect. You didn't directly feel anything in your wrists themselves during or after the freeze. But hands and fingers, even though they moved and felt normal, were rendered near-useless. You couldn't perform tasks such as gripping and pulling zippers or unfastening buttons. You needed help undressing.

Extreme cold also affected non-exposed private parts. I don't know where the expression "freezing your nuts off" came from, because on subzero days my tiny testicles scrambled up into my abdomen, sometimes not descending until roasting before an open fire.

Nature apologized for its harshness by producing displays of multi-sensory beauty. Below thirty below, wind and clouds were usually absent. The air was near-desert-dry except for tiny ice crystals that shimmered, suspended against the deep-blue, brilliant sky. (Someone in some other frigid place termed the effect, "diamond dust.") On rare occasions, the crystals aligned to prism light into "sun dogs," small, colored spots on both sides of the real sun. And at night, I'm certain I could have counted all 2,000 stars visible to the naked eye.

In the woods, frozen silence was sometimes interrupted by the echoing percussion of trees splitting open as their outer wood froze faster than their cores. Lake ice added moans, groans, and loud cracks as it expanded while freezing to four feet thick. And at fissures on large lakes, the tremendous pressure of section edges competing for the same space forced up ice ridges several feet high and hundreds of yards long.

We also created our own ephemeral ice art. At minus twenty and below, we spit upwards as high as we could, then watched the expectorations freeze and sometimes crackle and shatter before hitting the ground. Similarly, somewhere in the minus thirties, we could dramatically expand the effect by tossing water from a glass up into the air. And if we were willing to squander a nickel, we'd more-colorfully do same with a bottle of pop.

But no, when it was that cold, we did not write our names in the snow with yellow ink. We feared the legend of the kid, who somewhere, at some time had tried. And his member had flash-frozen and fallen off.

February 14, 1953: **Manufactured a snow tank.**

Street plows plus Dad's sidewalk shoveling had piled snow into a six-foot high, compact mound near the road. From the house side, I burrowed into the middle at ground level then scooped and hauled out snow to form a small igloo. Next, with the shaft of a broken hockey stick, I poked a couple of small openings overlooking the road. And last, I piled and shaped the excavated snow into a turret, lanced in the stick to simulate a cannon, crawled back inside, and spent the next couple of hours pretend-blasting passing cars.

February 23, 1953: **Witnessed a spectacular bumper-joring display.**

As I and a half dozen other kids got off the school bus at our common stop, fellow second-grader Duane Carlson scooted to the back of the vehicle, grabbed onto the bumper, dropped to a full squat and prepared for a brief boot-slide tow over the snow-packed street.

Duane really got caught up in the thrill ride. Literally. As the bus accelerated, something snagged his parka. Duane clutched the bumper with one hand as he desperately tried to extricate himself with the other.

We realized Duane was in trouble and held our breaths at the unfolding spectacle that confirmed our parents' warnings about the dangers inherent in the illicit activity. Fortunately, Duane was little enough and the snagging apparatus high enough that his head and upper body stayed above ground, rhythmically twisting from side to side as his legs and feet bounced and flopped like the road was a trampoline. In brief, rapid succession, his unzipped boots jettisoned from his feet.

Mercifully, before any of Duane's body parts followed his footwear, the bus reached its next stop, and he disengaged himself.

May 6, 1953: **Today was another blast.**

Though open-pit mining required sophisticated engineering, monstrous equipment, and monumental effort, the process was basic. Test bores determined areas to be mined. Land was cleared and overburden scraped off, exposing soft, rich "merch" ore that was scooped up and trucked away. Those initial depressions were then slowly expanded into terraced canyons hundreds of feet deep and covering thousands of acres.

Laborers spent weeks power drilling huge holes deep into the pits' walls. Specialists packed in explosives, and their carefully choreographed detonations sent a half million tons of iron-bearing rock at a time to the mine bottom. There, it was scooped up by power shovels, loaded into trucks, transported to crushers, and dropped into rail cars. At each pit, the process was repeated, usually for decades, until all ore had been removed.

Miners preparing blasting charges. (Iron Range Research Center)

Today was a scheduled blast day at a pit near us. Mom ritually removed a few items from her knick knack shelf, and precisely at noon the shock wave from the muffled boom rattled our windows. Dad had also taken a long-term precaution. When he built our house, he drywalled with two overlapping, perpendicular layers—the first nailed, the second glued—to ensure that seams wouldn't crack. As of 2014, after more than sixty years and hundreds of blasts, they hadn't. And won't.

June 13, 1953: **Took a chemical shower.**

I stared fascinated as a small plane buzzed the treetops down our street, a plume of thick, white smoke trailing from its tail. I ran inside and told Mom, who explained it was DDT being sprayed to get rid of army worms.

Last year the worms—technically, forest tent caterpillars—had stripped foliage from eleven-million acres of deciduous trees throughout northern Minnesota, including the Range. And in spite of the spraying campaign, this summer would end worse. The invaders would ultimately decimate twenty-six-million acres of trees. Caterpillars dropping on metal roofs sounded like rain. And vehicle-squashed worms layered so thick and slick on some roads that crews had to apply sand to keep driving surfaces safe.

June 19, 1953: **Ethel and Julius Rosenberg executed.**

I kind of understood that espionage was like serious sneaking and tattling. And I was familiar with the deliberate ending of life. I had watched Dad butcher farm animals and him and Grandpa B shoot game. But I struggled with the image of people having their heads shaved, then being strapped to a chair, capped with a sponge and hood, connected to heavy wires, and electrocuted. It seemed unnecessarily complicated and gruesome, especially after a classmate reported it had taken three jolts to kill Ethel, and that smoke had risen from her head.

July 9, 1953: **Suffered a new sensation.**

I led a neighborhood bike race and turned my head to trash-talk the losers behind me. However, I mouthed off too long and smashed full-speed into the rear bumper of a parked car I hadn't noticed. Momentum launched me to an excruciating testicle slam, my first, against the bike's handlebar stem. My competitors trash-talked my misfortune as they pedaled by.

July 29, 1953: **Didn't let sleeping dog lie.**

I hadn't met Mr. Webb and didn't yet comprehend the Cold War anxiety that prompted him to be the only homeowner in our neighborhood to construct a bomb shelter. It was just an unseen curiosity that made me turn my head and wonder what it looked like as I coasted by his house on my bike.

Mr. Webb also owned a black cocker spaniel, which normally napped in the side yard and barely raised its head when I rode by. But today, the dog shot across the grass and sank its teeth deep into the soft flesh behind my knee. Maybe the baseball card I had attached to flap against the spokes to mimic a motorbike sound provoked him.

I clenched back tears as Mom washed the wound then took me to the doctor for a tetanus shot.

August 16, 1953: **Temporarily played with temporary cousin.**

Nanna and Uncle Sam could not have children, so they were thrilled to reach the final stages of adopting a nine-year-old boy, who they brought up from Duluth to introduce to us. Uncle Sam was Swedish (his mother had emigrated to America from that country), so he and Nanna had worked with an agency in Minneapolis that specialized in placing American children of Swedish heritage. The organization had assured Nanna and Uncle Sam that Dennis was "perfect" and even looked like Uncle Sam.

Mom instructed me to be nice to my new cousin and to make him feel welcome. I did, even though I felt a twinge of envy when he carried in armfuls of new toys, including a huge, shiny fire engine. But maintaining nice became difficult. I couldn't understand Dennis; he talked funny. He also didn't share his toys and even shoved me a couple of times. But we made it through the afternoon, and I said, "See ya again," as he and his soon-to-be parents headed home.

Two months later, Mom said that Nanna and Uncle Sam were coming for another visit.

"What about Dennis?" I asked.

"Oh, he had all kinds of problems," Mom replied. "He was so mentally slow, he couldn't find his way the two blocks to school. He got into fights. And his speech impediment was so severe, the school couldn't help. So," she finished matter of factly, "Nanna and Uncle Sam returned him to the orphanage."

August 22, 1953: **Glowed with excitement.**

I was thrilled when Mom announced it was time to buy me a new pair of shoes. I didn't care about the footwear. I got to look at my bones.

At Ketolas, a salesman measured my feet, grabbed a box off a nearby shelf, and pulled out a pair of plain brown oxfords. I laced them on, stepped up onto a podium-shaped contraption the salesman called a fluoroscope, and slid my feet into a large slot at its base. The salesman then set a timer on the unit for twenty seconds, activated an X-ray, and he, Mom, and I peered into separate viewports. In the greenish glow, I could clearly see the bones of my feet and the outline of the shoes. The salesman instructed me to wiggle my toes then advised Mom there was plenty of room to grow into without raising blisters if I wore a double layer of socks.

September 20, 1953: **Enjoyed a double treat.**

Dad discovered a new radio western, *The Six Shooter*, and invited me to stay up past Sunday bedtime to listen with him. As I did on Saturdays during *Gunsmoke* broadcasts, I crawled onto his lap, and together we heard Jimmy Stewart quaver the first adventure of Texas plainsman Bret Ponset.

November 14, 1953: **Fondled my first fake butter.**

Grandma B assigned me a new kitchen task. She handed me a clear plastic bag full of white goo called oleomargarine. Near the center on one side was a red dot. Grandma instructed me to "pop the dot," then squeeze, knead and roll the bag until the red disappeared and inexplicably turned the soft, white mass yellow.

December 1, 1953: **Dad gifted Mom; she reciprocated.**

During the first year in the upstairs of our new, but not-quite-finished house, only our small bathroom had been privatized with a door. Today, Dad brought home an early Christmas gift for Mom, a door for their bedroom. Nine months later, my youngest sister Carolyn was born.

Dad installed remaining doors in privacy priority—sisters' bedroom, mine, and finally, closets—as funds became available.

Ill-Equipped

OUTSIDERS ROUTINELY UNDERSTATED that hockey on the Range approached religion. Approached?! Hell, we were a full-blown, out-in-the-open cult. And we practiced our ice rites with only four temporal objects: a pair of skates, a stick, and anything resembling a puck.

Now, one might wonder why a protective cup didn't top the list. Because as kids playing in the frigid outdoors, there wasn't much to protect. As the temperature dropped, our pea-size testicles sought warmth by climbing into our abdomens, and puny penises telescope-retracted. Plus, layered clothing cushioned us, at least from shoulders to knees, against whacks from sticks and pucks.

Skates were our absolute #1 necessity. Kids occasionally tried playing in street boots. But even on rough ice, a fast runner couldn't keep up with a slow skater, which often was me, especially during my first shifts on brand-new used skates. From previously owned pairs lined up on the worn pine floorboards at Grande Hardware, Dad would select an oversized set I could wear for a couple of seasons. I stuffed crumpled *Mesabi Daily News* pages into the extra space behind the toes and pulled on as many layers of socks as needed to fill other voids. Then when I eventually outgrew the leather boots, we swabbed them with shoe polish, returned to Grande, and traded in for another oversized, used, polished pair that, by the end of negotiations, cost two to three dollars. I skated on my final lineage-unknown blades until

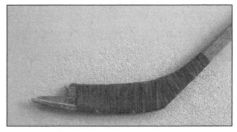

The author's hockey stick at season's end. (Author collection)

I was twenty-five, when I spent $39.95 for an out-of-the-box, perfect-fit pair of C.C.M. Mustangs.

In fact, until adulthood, I played with only one new piece of equipment, a stick, which I received ritually. Santa probably left other gifts, but I don't remember because there was only one reason to leap out of bed at first light Christmas morning. That was to run to the pristine Northland Pro that leaned upright against our fireplace next to my Christmas stocking. Its solid white-ash shaft was smoothly tenon-and-mortis joined to a straight, lacquered wood blade. It was beautiful.

But it would suffer serial abuse yet have to last until the next Christmas. So I reached into the toe of my Christmas stocking, pulled out the puck-size roll of black friction tape that Santa always tucked there, and wrapped the blade from tip to heel and back again.

But even with the double-wrap, the blade bottom gradually rasped raw. At each reappearance of wood, I wound additional tape over what remained of the previous layers. But eventually, the blade also split or snapped, at which time I attached wood or metal splints and again wrapped with more tape.

Dad once came up with a scheme to replace a mortally injured stick. His brainstorm formed during a high-school hockey tournament game at the Eveleth Hippodrome, three miles from home and one of the Range's two indoor rinks. For nearly thirty years the rudimentary, rectangular brick box, topped by a half-dome roof, had enclosed a naturally frozen ice surface. Then recently, the facility had been modernized with refrigeration units that allowed the creation of artificial ice over a concrete floor. Still, only the dressing rooms and an attached garage-size lobby were heated. The 3,000 spectators who packed onto bench bleacher seats generated enough body heat to stay warm, but their collective breath often froze on the inside of the outside walls. Late-comers relegated to the highest row had to lean forward to avoid contact.

The seating area was smoke-free, so during intermissions, the lobby became a nico-

The author at age twenty-five, skating on his first-ever pair of brand-new skates. (Ann Barfknecht)

tine den, with cravers lighting up, standing up shoulder to shoulder. Over the decades, smoking forests of Pall Malls, Chesterfields, and Lucky Strikes had precipitated an ochre patina on the walls and photos of Eveleth hockey legends. When someone opened a door to eject a butt, the cold blast for me was as relieving as a puff of oxygen to a one-lunged emphysemic.

Meanwhile, the ice was also being refreshed. As at outdoor high-school games, two junior-varsity players on skates spiraled around the rink with small wood hand plows and pushed their scrapings out end-board doors. Two men wearing rubber boots followed, each controlling a fifty-five-gallon drum filled with water and mounted upright on a self-propelled, hand-dolly-like contraption. A yard-wide strip of canvas attached to the tank bottom flattened out onto the ice, and a valve regulated a continuous supply of water to soak it. Like a large sponge mop applying a coat of wax, the wet pad transformed the skate-scarred ice smooth.

All area high-school season-finale hockey tournament games were played at the Hipp, and Dad, I, and sometimes Grandpa Stoltz attended as many as Dad's work schedule allowed. During one, it struck Dad that since losing players had no immediate need for their school-supplied sticks they might give one to me. So he directed me to ask.

Twice that evening, I reluctantly made my way down under the stands to the mouth of whichever chute funneled the losing team from ice to locker room. I looked up into the players' angry, dejected eyes and repeatedly blurted, "Can I have your stick? You don't need it anymore." Probably only because I was nine did I not actually get a stick that a proctologist would have had to remove. Instead, a few players just labeled me the orifice into which the stick would have been inserted.

So I continued to make do with one stick per season. But because I lived across the street from our hockey rink, I never wanted for pucks. The boards weren't topped by glass or wire screen, plus nature and plows piled snow around them. So, pucks deflected over the boards sometimes disappeared like clams in beach sand. We always went after them with stick blades but knew that if we didn't locate them quickly, we likely weren't going to so didn't bother for long.

When spring suns began melting snow, I made regular passes by our picture window to spot the return of the buried pucks. When a speck of black peeked out of the white snow, it absorbed the sun's rays and quickly melted the immediate surrounding area into a small display case. With each exposure, I ran across the street and plucked out the prize.

However, most players claimed continued ownership of their pucks by carving their initials into one or both faces. But like a cattle rustler, I altered some—such as Dennis Pietrini's (DP) and Charlie Lutkovich's (CL)—to my GB brand. The rest I distributed to their owners, a goodwill gesture I hoped might minimize "accidental" elbows to my nose when they played against me.

Shin bruises, however, were unavoidable. Hockey lore has it that players some icy-where protected the front of their lower legs with magazines. It wasn't us. We literally and figuratively played shinny hockey. Though we made every effort to keep stick blades and pucks on the ice, the lumber and rubber regularly whacked welts and bruises onto the thin skin covering our tibias.

The unprotected casing that enclosed our alleged intelligence sometimes suffered worse damage. Accidental high sticks and errant elbows and pucks broke noses, opened gashes, and loosened, chipped or knocked out teeth. And just about every one of us cracked our skulls on the ice, more than once, me included. Memories of my brain bangs are understandably fuzzy. Except once I'm pretty sure I thought I saw God.

And He held forth a Northland Pro.

<u>March 20, 1954</u>: **Took my first shot.**

Raised in a family and community of hunters, I had recently wondered when I'd get to to shoot a gun. But I didn't ask, knowing Dad would reply, "When it's time."

Today, as we walked in silence out of the woods after a typical hare-hunting session, Dad stopped, held out his single-shot, bolt action .22 rifle, and said, "Wanna try?" I nodded and reached for the new experience. Dad issued a couple of concise instructions, and I triggered my first bullet into a nearby stump.

The author's first gun, which was also his father's first gun. (Author collection)

Decades later I learned that when Dad was my age, his father had bought the Springfield .22 new for him. Howard, Sr., had then allowed Howard, Jr., to immediately hunt alone with it, but only within sight of home.

April 9, 1954: **Got my first look at television . . . sort of.**
Two television stations had recently powered up in Duluth, so Grandpa B bought a small tabletop set and invited Dad and me to watch the Friday night fights with him. Grandpa fiddled with a rabbit-ears antenna as we huddled in front of black-and-white ghosts floating through hissing snow. Only when the Gillette Cavalcade of Sports theme played, was I sure I had "watched" boxing.

May 19, 1954: **With a bun in the oven, we get a TV.**
On his way home from work, Dad picked up a twenty-one-inch Sylvania Halo Light television, a perk Mom had requested as company during her forthcoming home confinement with her fourth and final newborn. Dad positioned the imposing wood cabinet in the corner between our living room fireplace and picture window. After supper, he installed a roof antenna and at 8:30 clicked the set on. The picture tube and surrounding fluorescent light gradually glowed. As Dad twisted the horizontal and vertical hold control knobs to eliminate flickers, I heard familiar radio voices.

When the black-and-white images focused, I saw, for the first time, _My Little Margie's_ characters. But Margie, Vern, and Freddie didn't look like I had imagined. My vague disappointment repeated over the next week, when Miss Brooks, Chester Riley, and other radio friends also looked nothing like they had sounded.

June 10, 1954: **Scratched an itch with a penny.**
One set of the railroad tracks that webbed our city ran next to Grandpa Stoltz's house, a block from ours. Steam or sometimes diesel engines pulling a hundred iron-ore cars at a time regularly rumbled by.

Hearing one approaching, I finally gave in to a long-suppressed urge. I placed a penny on the shiny top of a rust-colored rail and ran to Grandpa's yard to watch. The coin disappeared under the first wheel of the 100-ton locomotive. After waving to the conductor in the red, wood caboose a couple of minutes later, I returned to the tracks. In the cinders next to the rail, Abe Lincoln grimaced from a quarter-size, paper thin, copper disc.

Here Today, Where Tomorrow?

June 18, 1954

A s a nine-year-old, I had no idea I was about to experience the remarkable rebirth of both a town and an industry. I was simply excited at the prospect of spending a week with Mom's oldest brother, Uncle Charlie, and his wife, Delores, forty miles away in their newly built home in Babbitt.

Upon arriving, I found Babbitt bewildering. I had seen many new houses go up between, next to, or near established residences throughout the Queen City and expected Uncle Charlie's setting to be similar. But his home was completely surrounded by other newly constructed houses, schools, churches, stores, streets, sidewalks, and parks. The entire town looked as though it had just been created, all at once.

It had.

That alone didn't make Babbitt unique on the Range, however. During the first few decades of iron mining, several hundred "locations" had come into similar almost-instant existence throughout the Mesabi. Most often, mining companies set up the clusters of homes at the edge of new pits and rented them affordably to employees, who then walked to work. Larger, independent, incorporated villages and cities also developed as population centers plus hubs of service and commerce.

All directly or indirectly existed at the whim of mining companies, which owned almost all of the Mesabi's land or mineral rights under it. When they decided to expand an existing pit or start a new dig, everyone who resided or conducted business where ore would be removed was informed they had to move. Or conversely, when a mine tapped out and there was no longer a need for a nearby location, it ceased to exist.

But structures were not routinely demolished or abandoned. Many were recycled. Companies sometimes transferred houses to newly established locations. Or renters might be offered the option to purchase their homes for one dollar and pay to relocate them to private property of their choosing. Speculators and investors, too, bought and moved houses for resale. Some buildings were cannibalized for their components.

The Village of Franklin, which abutted the City of Virginia, staged one of the largest disappearing acts. When I first accompanied Dad to the Queen City, Franklin comprised four major and more than a half dozen small locations, each named after the mine it served. Ten years later, after those pits had continually expanded then merged, all that remained of Franklin were three dozen residents in eleven homes lining a one-block extension of the east end of Virginia's main downtown street.

At times, companies determined it was in their best interest to re-stabilize disrupted labor forces and residents by literally picking up and moving entire towns. The Village of Aurora, for instance, incorporated in 1903 but too close to a mine and too far from a railroad. So two years later, the homes of all 174 residents plus every business structure was hauled a mile south. Nearly forty years later, a lake near the village was drained and the Embarrass River diverted to get at more ore.

In 1907 an Oliver Mining Company test bore tapped into a rich vein beneath the Village of Sparta. So in 1908, the town—at the time, one of the Range's largest—began a two-year, two-mile transfer of its 1,000 residents plus department store, butcher shop, blacksmith, barbershop, boardinghouses, saloons, and other businesses to Gilbert.

The most ambitious relocation involved the Range's largest population center, Hibbing. In 1915, when Oliver Mining again found ore under a main street, the company and city fathers negotiated the move of all of the town's 20,000 residents, plus 185 houses and two dozen businesses. The company promised to finance not only the conveyance but also construction of new public buildings. Planning for the maneuver three miles south to the small village of Alice took four years. Hibbing was then transferred structure by structure over the next two years at a cost of sixteen-million dollars (about $200 million in 2010 dollars). And as agreed, Oliver built new facilities, including a hotel, hospital, village hall, and a four-million-dollar, castle-like high school, said to be the country's finest at the time. The transplant then annexed its village host and renamed the new entity, City of Hibbing. The ore beneath Hibbing's former site was subsequently removed to ultimately help form the world's largest open pit iron mine.

The moves were spectacular undertakings. Huge jacks lifted houses, most made of wood, then lowered them onto specially built, large, flatbed, trucks. The abodes then slowly rolled and rocked to their new site, usually with their furniture and sometimes residents inside. Reportedly, even a baby was delivered while its mother was being delivered. Sometimes even the dead were raised. The occupants of stray graves, such as around churches, were scooped up with steam shovels, then relocated to new resting places.

Large buildings, such as Sparta's high school, were sectioned, transported, then rejoined. Some structures were skidded during the winter. At least one didn't make it. During Hibbing's move, an off-balance hotel tumbled from its truck and splintered beyond salvaging.

Major relocations halted not long after the end of World War II. The number of expandable pits dwindled, and there was nowhere to start new ones. The seventy-million tons of ore each year that had ended up as military hardware had just about exhausted the Range's rich, relatively easy-to-extract and -process hematite.

As a kid, I had no awareness that we Rangers faced an uneasy, uncertain future.

Others, however, had known from the earliest days that our finite high-grade lode would eventually be depleted. They also knew that the Range was replete with low-grade taconite that contained even more iron than the hematite deposits. Trouble was, the lean, hard rock was extremely challenging to mine economically and process into usable ore. Scientists and mining companies had been trying for decades.

The world's first commercial taconite processing plant, in fact, set up in 1922 at a desolate wilderness area at the northeastern tip of the Mesabi. The small, independent operation also established a crude, self-contained town for their workers and named it Babbitt. The exposed, gray taconite there made removal easier then elsewhere, but the plant could not concentrate it into a product satisfactory to steel mills, so failed and shut down in 1924. Babbitt and the hope taconite held out were left to die.

But the University of Minnesota's School of Mines and a few large corporations persisted in efforts to turn taconite mining profitable. They succeeded, and a few years after the war's end, the companies began building large-scale taconite plants around the Range. Reserve Mining Company, one of the first, announced that they would re-open the mine near the remains of Babbitt, construct a crusher, and ship the ore fifty miles by rail to a processing plant they would erect on the shore of Lake Superior. Reserve also said they would build a town from scratch for the 1,000 employees who would work at the mine and crusher. Babbitt was about to become the Range's only resurrected town. (Taconite also spawned two pre-planned newborns: Silver Bay, site of Reserve's plant, and Hoyt Lakes, established by Erie Mining Company.)

Reborn Babbitt was conceived on desks at a Chicago engineering firm. The drawings came to life in 1952 when the first houses, prefabricated in nearby Biwabik, were trucked in on double trailers. Several different floor plans were available, yards were spacious, payments were less than fifty dollars per month, and no down payment was required. Reserve also paid for construction of infrastructure—utilities, paved streets, sidewalks, and sewers—plus schools and commercial retail buildings. And finally, the company landscaped it all. Babbitt was completed just before my visit.

As a civil engineer for Reserve, Uncle Charlie was involved in all phases of Babbitt's planning and development. Shortly before my visit, he and Aunt Delores had moved from Duluth to the town he had helped design and build. I spent a week with them in the Range's future.

Our family wouldn't be directly caught up in the taconite revolution for another fifteen years, however, until Dad's standard Enterprise Mine, just north of the Queen City, tapped out and closed for good. His employer, M.A. Hanna, had, however, established a taconite mine and plant, thirty-five miles away, near Keewatin. So after driving six miles round-trip to work for nearly two decades, Dad commuted seventy miles daily the remaining ten years of his career.

But we didn't have to move.

June 28, 1954: Undamaged after butt-ugly slide.

Yesterday, I cobbled together a shack on a vacant lot, a block away near Grandpa Stoltz's house. I spent the morning hauling boards in my wagon from a couple of abandoned, dilapidated turn-of-the-century sheds a few blocks east. After lunch, I leaned and layered the scavenged scraps into a cubbyhole clubhouse.

Today, I invited a couple of friends inside. Not long after, soft rain began to fall. My humble hut soon featured running water, prompting my guests to check out early.

Determined to stop the leaks, I shinnied up an adjacent tree for an aerial survey. Suddenly, I slip-shot down the wet trunk to the main fork, where a thumb-size stub rammed up my rectum.

Because of lucky alignment and insertion shielded by clothing, my colon was not scraped, let alone perforated. In fact, the sensation was only the mild discomfort I would experience again at my first prostate exam forty years later. I did, however, have to perform some unusual maneuvers to extract pants and underwear. And after several days with no bowel movement, I came perilously close to telling my parents. But everything did come out all right in the end.

July 16, 1954: **Avoided an explosive situation.**

I had played with new neighbors Russell and David Graves for nearly a week before asking them why I hadn't seen their dad. He worked in Indiana, they explained, and was only able to come home on weekends.

A couple of hours later, their father pulled up in a red moving-van-size truck. Large, white block letters stenciled onto both sides of the box spelled, "DYNAMITE." I figured the truck was empty but still didn't play near the Graves' house on weekends.

July 30, 1954: **Received a redundant reward.**

My four-day stay at Bible camp included a competition to see which one of us kids could memorize the most Bible verses. For half an hour each evening, we sat cross-legged on the floor in front of an adult moderator. In his lap he held a small, black wood box, with a small red light centering the top. When a contestant recited a Bible verse correctly, the bulb blinked.

Providentially, I had participated in a similar contest six weeks before, at a summer Bible school during a stay with my aunt and uncle in Babbitt. Two weeks later, I had repeated the exercise at our church's Bible school.

Memory momentum carried me to easy victory. The red light flashed nearly nonstop as I obliterated the competition. After the sessions, though, I sometimes wondered how the inanimate box knew whether a recitation was correct or not. Didn't matter though because, during closing ceremonies, I accepted first prize. A new Bible.

August 6, 1954: **Mesmerized by moving bridge**

Uncle Sam drove us down the steep hill from their house to my favorite Duluth attraction, the aerial lift bridge.

The Duluth Lift Bridge. (Minnesota Historical Society)

The high-profile web of steel girders, trusses and crossbeams formed a 225-foot-high inverted "U" over a canal that separated the world's longest freshwater sand bar, Park Point, from the city. Connecting the bases of the erector-set bridge's uprights was a 390-foot-long section of Lake Avenue, which carried Point residents and beach-goers over the channel. That roadway was also regularly lifted and lowered by huge concrete counterweights plus electrically powered pulleys and cables in the end support towers.

Reason was, the canal was a conduit for boat traffic, including massive freighters, between Lake Superior and Duluth Harbor. As often as a couple of dozen times daily during the shipping season, the long-short-long-short blast from a ship would signal a request to raise the road. The bridge's horn would copy the signal back as acknowledgment. Then, as the vessel approached, a trilling bell warned pedestrians, gates closed to stop vehicles, and the rudimentary mechanisms hoisted the roadway a foot a second.

Freighters, some 600 feet long, then entered the quarter-mile-long, concrete-walled channel and slowly passed through, seemingly almost within touching distance. Uncle Sam lifted and held me atop the ledge on our side. Each ship's wake surged then slapped against the cement, and the crew members who leaned over their metal deck rails waved, I was sure, directly at me.

I had no idea and didn't care what cargo—iron ore, grain, limestone, coal—the freighters carried to or from the loading docks, elevators, stockpiles, and production facilities that lined the harbor. Uncle Sam said ships often entered with one product beneath their rows of sealed deck hatches and left with another.

I wondered what it was like working on the ships. Nine years later, I had a one-time opportunity to find out. But I turned it down for a one-time opportunity to work as a lifeguard at an all-girls camp. The decision was agonizing.

August 7, 1954: **Came back coal black.**

Nanna sent me four blocks up the hill behind their house to fill a pan with wild strawberries that grew along railroad tracks there. I returned with the fruit that, along with most of me, was black from soot that had settled the area from coal-stoked steam locomotives.

August 8, 1954: **Uncle Charlie died, mysteriously.**

Nanna hung up the phone, turned to Uncle Sam and me, and sighed, "My brother's dead."

Uncle Charlie and Aunt Delores had boated to an island in Birch Lake, near Babbitt, for a picnic. According to Aunt Delores, their boat drifted from shore. Uncle Charlie, an excellent swimmer who served in the Seabees during World War II, went after it. She said that when he reached the boat, he yelled he couldn't hang on and slipped beneath the surface.

His body was recovered and, in spite of a large, inexplicable bruise on his head, Aunt Delores would not authorize an autopsy. Shortly after the funeral, she got rid of all of his, their, and even her possessions and moved to Florida. Three months later, she married a night-club pianist.

August 29, 1954: **Family completed.**

Mom gave birth to our final family member, Carolyn Sue.

September 7, 1954: **Revised rote.**

Our first fourth-grade assignment upon returning to school was to relearn our daily opening recitation of the Pledge of Allegiance. Miss Bezek explained that, during the summer, President Eisenhower had signed a law that added the words "under God," between "one nation" and "indivisible."

September 15, 1954: **New neighbor is spectacular.**

I got my first nighttime look at U.S. Steel's experimental taconite plant. The company had recently started up the huge addition to their already massive Rouchleau crusher, which loomed over Ridgewood on the east. The new-

Rouchleau crusher and experimental taconite plant. (W.A. Fisher Co., Virginia Area Historical Society)

tech "agglomerator" digested and concentrated flour-fine, low-grade taconite fed to it by conveyors. Jets of burning oil then fused that higher-grade product into clumps that were dropped into railroad cars.

In the darkness, the monster appeared to breathe fire.

October 2, 1954: **Auto repair as spectator sport.**

Most miners maintained and repaired their own cars. Not Grandpa B. I had never seen him so much as pop the hood and check the oil dipstick. And I recognized early on that I had inherited his auto aversion. But I liked accompanying Grandpa to Bill's Sinclair Service Station around the corner from his Mt. Iron home, where he paid to have his Mercury looked after.

Bill's had a hydraulic lift, so I could surveil the mysteries of a car's under-belly without sliding on my back. And Bill, himself, wore a stare-at skull cap that, like the creases in his being, was grease-infused.

Best of all was the "slider" pop-vending machine. As during every visit, today Grandpa B handed me a nickel, and I opened the lid of the chest-type compartment to expose bottles of Nesbitt's products hanging from six metal tracks. I slid an orange to the end of one, plunked in the coin to release a small, locked gate, and pulled out my six-ounce treat.

Later, I surgically removed the bottle cap's cork lining in one piece with my pocket knife and positioned it inside my t-shirt. I then placed the metal cap over it on the outside and pressed them back together to form a badge.

October 23, 1954: **Extinguished a burning desire to smoke.**

While exploring a brushy field next to the recently closed airport, Mike Nadolske and I discovered a patch of plants topped with cone-shaped clusters of tiny, dry, brown petals. They looked like tobacco, we agreed. So we picked one and returned to my garage. Out of sight inside, we stripped off the petals, and I rolled them in a shred of newspaper. I placed the stogie between my lips, and Mike lit it.

I took a tentative, tiny toke, which stoked the paper to flames but fortunately didn't singe my lips or lungs. I dropped the flaming mass onto the cement floor and we stomped it out.

November 13, 1954: **Witnessed grease converted to soap.**

In a cast-iron kettle, Grandma B warmed a chunk of beef tallow delivered by son Wilson, a butcher. Grandpa B brought in a small wood bucket holding homemade lye. He had placed ashes from his burning barrel into a box atop an inclined, baffled wood chute and drenched them with water. The liquid had seeped, drained, and strained into the container.

Grandma added the lye to the melted fat and stirred while the mixture cooled. When she determined the temperature was right, she poured the liquid soap into a cake pan. After it had solidified, she cut it into bars, then shaved them as needed to do laundry.

November 25, 1954: **Grandpa administers uplifting safety seminar.**

After Thanksgiving dinner, my cousin Wilson "Butch" Barfknecht and I sneaked away from Grandpa B's Mt. Iron house for a look into the Oliver mining pit, a block away. As we peered over the edge, someone levitated us by our coat collars. It was Grandpa, who—while dangling us back to his house—delivered a stern lecture on the dangers of playing so close to the chasm.

December 27, 1954: **Dad's eats spoiled our appetites.**

After choking down army chow—including "stew" steeped from garbage in garbage cans—during his four-year World War II excursion through Africa and Europe, Dad appreciated just about all civilian food. Today, that included a snack of blood sausage washed down with buttermilk. He didn't say where he got the nearly black meat. Mom and I wished only that he hadn't. Neither of us could stomach the concept of ingesting congealed pig's blood. And we had sampled buttermilk and agreed it tasted like vomit. Which we tried not to do while watching Dad savor his treats.

You May Think It's Funny,
But It'Snot

As POINT MEN IN THE DEFENSE against winters' bitter assaults, our noses near-continuously generated fluid to warm and moisten arctic-cold, desert-dry air headed for our lungs. Mission accomplished, it was then discharged.

Early on, as with other emissions, our mothers took care of the mess by wiping with cotton handkerchiefs. When we turned three, our moms began tucking the hankies into our shirt or pants pockets. But we rarely pulled them out, preferring to swipe on the backs of our mittens or coat and shirt sleeves. By about fourth grade, however, the resulting streaks became an embarrassment akin to wetting your pants. But we still didn't deploy the designated cloths, opting instead for our "Finnlander handkerchiefs."

Now, about that name. For reasons too historically and culturally involved to go into, of the forty-some ethnic groups that had settled the Range, Finns ended up being singled out as the butt of jokes, albeit by my time with no underlying animosity. That included, at some point, someone tagging our nose-evacuation technique with the "Finnlander" prefix.

The method is not unique to the Range. It's primal and probably universal.

Still, Rangers deserve naming rights, because we perfected the technique. The development parallels Range hockey. Consistently, the legions of kids who played that game multiplied by the extensive ice time they logged resulted in more college, Olympic and professional hockey players per capita skating out of the Range than any other region south of the Canadian border. Similarly, the tens of thousands of Rangers each forced to clear their noses several hundred times every winter also produced a like percentage of hot-shot snot-shots.

So to me, "Finnlander handkerchief" is neither humorous or pejorative. It's downright honorific and puts Finns right up there with Henry J. Heimlich.

And like the good doctor's windpipe-clearing maneuver, the Finnlander handkerchief is straightforward and not appetizing to watch. You hold an index finger of one hand tight against the nostril on the same side, then clear the opposite, open nostril with a forceful closed-mouth blow. Repeat with the opposite hand and nostril.

Though simple, the technique required years of practice to discharge efficiently and neatly. During our rookie seasons, we bent over at the waist, so gravity ensured that no matter how disastrous our efforts, the results headed to the ground, not onto chins or parka fronts. We gradually straightened up and then even leaned backwards, moving our torsos rapidly forward and snapping our heads at the last second to add velocity and distance. The quick release also ensured a compact nugget, not a stream or spray. And ultimately, we'd squeeze off two clean shots, one nostril followed quickly by the other.

We male kids used the method openly and almost exclusively. Most adult males, on the other hand, used their Finnlander handkerchiefs discretely, like in the woods or mine pits.

And only once did I witness a Queen City female—openly and perfectly—finger her Finnlander handkerchief. The wool-shirted, bib-overalled, toque-topped, sturdy stub swaggered out of Sam and Buck's bar, shot a pair of loogies at a parking meter, then lit up a Lucky.

Perfection isn't always pretty.

January 19, 1955: **One mystery about girls solved.**

I blurted to Miss Bezek that I was about to throw up, so she rushed me across the hall into the girls' bathroom. I was in no condition to be embarrassed, plus I had occasionally wondered what the female facilities looked like. Not much different than ours, I discovered between wretches. Same porcelain sinks, black and white tiled floors, and frosted-glass window. The only obvious difference was no urinals but more stalls.

February 6, 1955: **Dad said my play was off target.**

During my bath, I shot miniature plastic bullets at a floating Ivory soap bar from my toy torpedo boat. After drying off and putting on flannel pj's, I carried the plastic craft into my bedroom and set it in on the floor. Also on the floor, across the room, was a model house I had built with my American Plastic Bricks kit. I had assembled the interlocking red bricks and accessories—white operating doors and windows, green cardboard roof panel, and chimney—into a self-designed replica of our small, uncomplicated ranch.

In a spasm of destructive curiosity, I repeatedly fired tiny torpedos at it. The hard projectiles slammed the structure, chipping bricks as they knocked out sections at the roofline and around doors and windows. I had just about shot the new-build to a rubble of original pieces when Dad moved into my doorway.

"You should build, not destroy," he said.

"I know," I responded contritely while thinking, *but damn, demolition is fun.*

February 24, 1955: Schoolmate suffers unique hockey injury.

As our bus-stop group assembled near the hockey rink, Charlie L. hopped over the low boards and slid-walked to one of the goals, fashioned from iron pipe and chicken wire. He grabbed the top cross member with both hands, and swung—with both boots sliding on the ice—in and out of the metal cage. Suddenly, his feet shot up full-frontal horizontal, gravitating Charlie back and down in embrace with the net. As the back of Charlie's head smacked the ice, the goal's top pipe kissed him hard, knocking out a top front tooth.

A few days later, a dentist filled the gap with a silver prosthetic that Charlie flashed for years.

March 27 & 28, 1955: Snow packs unexpected impact.

On an unusually balmy forty-three-degree Sunday, a half dozen of us boys divided into two squads and built separate snow forts facing each other at close quarters. Each crew of combat engineers maneuvered massive balls of sticky snow into a U-shaped base then rolled, lifted, and fit smaller balls on top. A third layer of even-smaller rolls finished the fortresses high enough to crouch behind, low enough to stand and throw over. And finally, we mortared snow into the outside gaps and used shovels to shear off the inside walls straight up and down.

We then manufactured and stockpiled ammunition. The objective of the forthcoming battle would be to destroy the enemy's fort from the top down, and the most efficient, destructive weapon was a snowball as dense and compact as you could squeeze to softball size. We limited each team's cache to thirty, verified, then headed home.

Next afternoon after school, we exchanged volleys. Our opponents' missiles inflicted far more damage than ours, and when Jimmy mistimed a standup and got smacked on his nose, we discovered why. We picked up the snowball, which hadn't disintegrated on impact as it should have. It was a "soaker." Our adversaries had snuck back last night with a pail of water, dipped their ammo, and removed it to freeze into rock-hard ice balls.

As Jimmy held a fragment of our former fortress against his nose to stop the bleeding, we hurled the soaker and our last two powder puffs, then surrendered. The other squad charged and finished destroying our fort with their hands and feet. Except for the indestructible base. We all laughed, then joined forces to destroy the other fort. Except for the indestructible base, traces of which along with ours would remain into May.

April 9, 1955: **No escape for Ralph and Alice.**

Jackie Gleason's _The Honeymooners_ was a funny skit, but watching it also made made me uncomfortable. The Kramdens' third-floor apartment felt so claustrophobic. Sure, I knew acquaintances who lived in equally cramped quarters. But they were at ground level. And they could step out into open spaces and woods, not concrete. The Kramdens seemed trapped. No wonder they continually bickered.

May 25, 1955: **Dad gave competitor the shaft.**

Dad chuckled as he set his lunchpail down on the kitchen table and hung up his engineer-style work hat. Mom and I snapped up our heads in unison. Dad rarely smiled, let alone audibly expressed amusement, especially after work.

Dad related that while scooping surface ore, the bucket of his power shovel had broken through into a small, uncharted underground mine that, a quick investigation revealed, connected via a tunnel to a competitor's nearby open-pit workings. That company—with no public explanation of how the errant excavation came to be—subsequently calculated the amount of ore they had removed and compensated Dad's company, M.A. Hanna, for it.

June 14 1955: **Reenie fell innocent victim.**

My middle sister stood by me as Larry Hunsinger and I fired verbal darts across the alley at each other. Suddenly, Larry picked up and hurled an Irish-cobbler-size rock. The stone potato cold-cocked Reenie right between the eyes and flipped her backwards onto the ground. But remarkably, the primitive weapon didn't cut her.

Aggravated by the ruckus, Dad came around the corner of our garage and shouted, "What the hell's going on?!"

Larry's, "I'm sorry. I meant to hit Gary," apology-explanation plus Reenie's lack of blood-letting evidently satisfied Dad, because without further words, he, Larry, and I resumed whatever we were doing before the altercation.

Reenie, on the other hand, spent the rest of the day holding dishcloth-wrapped ice cubes against her forehead.

June 16, 1955: **Combat foundation is short-lived.**

The hole for a new-build basement was dug this morning, which meant we neighborhood boys would have a brief opportunity to clay fight. So after lunch, a dozen of us gathered, split up, and lined up on the red-streaked, blue clay mounded on opposite sides of the excavation. For the next half hour, we molded the malleable material into golf-ball-size projectiles and pegged them at each other across the divide.

As always, our ammo dumps then dried overnight, lost color, and crumbled.

June 22, 1955: **Played with Grandma's undies.**

Grandma B stood five feet tall, rarely weighed less than 250 pounds, and sometimes spun hospital laundry-scale needles to 350. She attributed her condition to the onset of an untreatable metabolic condition at puberty.

All of her oversize clothes had to be handmade, including her cotton underwear. When a trio of her bloomers were pinned to the clothesline in a stiff breeze, it was like seeing the _Nina_, _Pinta_, and _Santa Maria_ in full sail. Which gave me an idea.

Many of us neighborhood boys made homemade parachutes. We tied four equal-length strings, one each to the corners of any square scrap of cloth we could scavenge. One of Dad's blue-and-white handkerchiefs from the rag pile, for instance, was ideal. We then tied all the string ends to a metal nut. After folding the cloth around a rock and winding the strings and nut around that package we threw it into the air as high as we could. When properly prepared, the nut unrolled the strings at apogee, the rock dropped out, and the parachute floated to the ground.

Tommy had recently been the envy of the neighborhood by floating a beautiful canopy made with a silk handkerchief donated by or appropriated from his grandmother. I couldn't rival its elegance, so I went for size. I smuggled a pair of Grandma's pink bloomers home and engineered a chute from them. It unfurled perfectly and blotted out the sun.

July 9, 1955: **Grandpa B launches local lore.**

Grandpa B never said why he had convinced Grandma to join him on the maiden voyage of his small, homemade wood rowboat. But he had, then maneuvered her down the steep hill from their cabin, onto the dock, and into the craft.

But the boat's planking hadn't yet swelled tightly together, and as they shoved off, Grandma's substantial mass helped force the lake up through the gaps. Just yards into the cruise, the vessel filled to the seat bottoms, rendering it impossible to row.

So Grandpa slipped into the armpit-deep water and pushed his swamped embarrassment back to shore as grinning neighbors watched, then picked up their phones to publicize.

The Thunder Mug

July 16, 1955

I SOMETIMES WONDERED WHY GRANDPA B'S lake was named after a snot rag. But I didn't ask. And I didn't notice that Grandma never visited the outhouse at their cabin there. I'm glad I didn't.

In the late 1940s, Grandpa leased a small parcel of vacant land from his employer, Oliver Mining Company, on the west shore of Hanky Lake, not far from his Mt. Iron home, which he also rented from Oliver. In the Land of 10,000 Lakes, Hanky was a metaphorical drop of snot, a shallow, fifty-acre glacial kettle hole. Expansive patches of lily pads, reeds, and cattails encroached from shore, and stumps, logs, limbs, and other natural debris littered the muck bottom.

I didn't care. I loved being with Grandpa and Grandma at Hanky Lake.

My visits began at age four, when Dad brought me along to help Grandpa construct a rustic cabin. Dad and Grandpa framed the one-room structure with uniform lower trunks of spruce they cut from the woods behind Grandpa's lot. They nailed rough-sawn pine boards to those pole studs and rafters, then covered all with sand-colored asphalt shingles.

The outside walls were also the inside walls. The interior was not insulated or finished. A small kitchen-area window framed a view of the Sandgrens' year-round home, a few hundred yards north. And a pair of windows eyed east over the lake to the year-round home of fellow First Covenant Church attendees, the Johnsons. For light after dark, Grandpa placed and hung kerosene lanterns. He hauled cooking and drinking water from home in a ten-gallon cylindrical metal container with a push-button spigot at the bottom.

Grandpa also constructed a crude outhouse, a claustrophobic one-holer. Knots that had fallen out of the siding boards provided light and ventilation. Tall timothy grass lined the twenty-yard path to it, and when heavy with seed, the bent-over tips tickled my face. I gave no thought to the concept that Grandma would have had a difficult time getting there and back, let alone in, on, off, and out.

The cabin's furnishings included a wood cook stove; a dishpan-size sink that drained via a scrap piece of hose onto the grass outside; an ice-box refrigerator; a small wood table and four chairs; two beds, a double and a twin; and a couple of wood rocking chairs.

Most fascinating to me was what was called the "slop pail," which sat on the floor between the ice box and the only entry door. The black-metal, five-gallon bucket with a hinged handle *was* a receptacle for slop—a slurry of water and mostly recognizable stuff, such as coffee grounds, apple cores, and other scraps.

Dozens of timber matches typically floated on top, most from Grandpa's ongoing efforts to keep his corncob pipe lit. He had tacked a piece of sandpaper above the pail so he could conveniently scratch a match, suck the flame into his pipe bowl, then drop-douse the burning stick into the liquid with a brief hiss. After Grandpa had eventually turned his *Field & Stream* to ashes, he'd dislodge them into the pail by rapping the pipe bowl on the rim. The container also served as a spittoon for his spent Copenhagen snoose. A couple of times a day, Grandpa emptied the pail down the outhouse hole, then rinsed and recharged it with lake water.

Because their cabin was crude and close to home, Grandma and Grandpa rarely overnighted there. When I learned they planned to, I practically begged to stay with them. They usually said yes, including today, when Dad drove me to Hanky Lake for my first sleep-over of the summer.

Grandpa had left to get a block of ice for the fridge, Grandma was darning socks, and Dad couldn't stay. So I set out solo to thin Hanky's panfish population. From under the twin bed, I pulled out the thin, round Copenhagen can that held my beginner's collection of hooks, swivels, catgut leaders, and split-shot sinkers. I slid the tackle box into my pants pocket, pulled on my straw hat, grabbed Grandpa's coffee can containing worms, then skidded down the steep, brushy bank that dropped to his wood dock.

A nine-foot-long bamboo cane pole lay across the planks, ready for action. From its tip, an attached six-foot length of black fishline passed through a red-and-white wood bobber, then connected to a tiny snell hook via swivel and clear leader. I pulled out a wiggling worm, pinched off a half-inch section, threaded it onto the hook, then—as Grandpa had tutored—spit on it for luck.

It worked. After every bobber lob to the edge of nearby lily pads, bluegills raced sunfish to the bait, sometimes seemingly even before it rippled the surface. I'd yank the flopping winner out of the water and, if it was a rare "keeper," unhook it into a wire-mesh live box.

When Grandpa returned, he shouted from above, "Hey, Buckshot, are there any left for me to catch?" He then joined me, pipe in mouth, fly rod in hand until Grandma summoned us to supper.

Afterwards, while Grandma heated lake water then did dishes, Grandpa rowed us counterclockwise around the lake in his small, homemade wood boat. During the circuit, we used metal rods with open-face reels to cast minnows near crappie hangouts such as sunken trees or brush. Grandpa held his pole with his left hand and used his right to continually re-light his pipe. I held my pole in my right hand and used my left to continually bail the leaky water craft. We returned at sunset with a stringer of crappies. And I had caught more than Grandpa, because my spit had splattered better luck, I figured.

We headed up to the fish-cleaning station, near the outhouse. There, Grandpa grabbed a wide board that leaned against the privy and laid it across the top of his "burning barrel," a rusty fifty-five-gallon drum that consumed combustible waste. Next, he briefly disappeared into the cabin, lit kerosene lamps, brought one out, and set it on one end of the plank. He then scaled the crappies with a large metal spoon and removed heads and innards with his fish knife and hands. Moths, June bugs, and other insects attracted to the light, swarmed around Grandpa's operation, which he interrupted only to swat mosquitoes. An ensemble of croaking frogs and chirping crickets accompanied Grandpa's rhythmic spoon scrapes and intermittent slaps. From around the lake, creaking springs on opening wood screen doors and their loud claps shut added to the surround-sound.

We rinsed the fish flesh and our hands in the lake then put our cleaned catches in the ice box. Grandpa pulled out a Fitgers, handed me a Nesbitt's, and we sat down with Grandma, in her tent nightgown, shuffling playing cards at the table. She had removed her dentures and placed them in a glass on a kitchen shelf, where they grinned at me until she reinstalled them next morning. By lamplight, we then dealt hands of canasta and smear, with rules altered so that three—including a ten-year-old—could play. And Grandpa played his usual game within the games. He let me win a couple of times. And he toyed with Grandma, letting her lead until sometimes the last hand of a game, before decimating her. After again doing so on the final hand of our final game,

Grandma slapped her cards down on the table while moaning, "Ah, sheeeeeeit, Paul!" Without teeth, the "sh" hissed like a punctured tire, and Grandma sustained the "e's" before gumming the "it" as a separate, accented syllable.

Grandpa patted her hand, got up, and grabbed a flashlight. I accompanied him to the outhouse. Grandma was in bed when we returned and, as Grandpa extinguished the lanterns, I crawled under the covers of the twin bed while adding my voice to the "See ya in the mornin'" refrain.

I awoke to the aroma of the wood stove frying potatoes. Grandma, teeth in, had also dusted our fish with seasoned flour and was frying them in butter. As she set her dishes on the table, Grandpa entered with a fresh slop pail and a fistful of green onions plucked just outside the door. The fish backbones and ribs pulled out of the cooked flesh as a unit. Still, we chewed gingerly to avoid lancing a rogue bone needle into our gums or throats. Grandpa and I also dipped the green onions into salt, then bit off the white bottoms.

Minutes after we finished, Mom pulled up to take me home via church. As I headed out the door, I dropped my onion tops into the slop pail.

* * * *

Some fifty years later, I set out to revisit Hanky Lake, but couldn't remember how to get there. I consulted a map and was surprised to see it spelled, "Haenke." Turns out the lake was not named after a handkerchief, but rather a surveyor for the Oliver Mining Company, Mr. Haenke, who lived at his namesake.

Also, while reminiscing with my Uncle Wilson around the same time, I found out that the slop pail had contained more crap than I had known. Grandma had also somehow used it as her toilet, an image I immediately repressed. That explained three things: why I never saw her go to the outhouse, why she occasionally invented errands that required me to leave the cabin, and why Grandpa sometimes referred to the receptacle as the "thunder mug."

July 25, 1955: **Rite of passage felt wrong.**

Like most Range men, Dad was not publicly demonstrative. At home, however, my sisters and I jockeyed to sit on his lap and be cuddled. Dad hugged and kissed us goodnight, and when we were nearby, we hugged and kissed him goodbye as he left for work.

Today, Dad drove me to our church, where we met up with the family that would carpool me to a week at Bible camp. Dad placed my suitcase in their trunk then turned and silently faced me. I wanted to kiss him goodbye, and I think he wanted to kiss me.

Instead, I awkwardly thrust out my hand. Dad cocked his head slightly, nodded with a faint smile, and shook it. I felt a bit more manly but didn't like it.

And I never kissed Dad goodbye again. Until his funeral.

August 2, 1955: **Dennis's swing was really foul.**

I saw Dennis coming at me down the street carrying a baseball bat in his left hand and dangling a wiggling mouse by the tail in his right. Without warning, he tossed the rodent high into the air, grabbed the bat with both hands, and line-drived the executed mouse within inches of me.

Dennis laughed. Didn't seem funny to me.

August 13, 1955: **Got stoned.**

Something I did or said provoked my playmates to chase me home while pegging marble-size rocks. I ran faster scared than they did mad. But a couple of their missiles caught up to the back of my head and opened small but bloody cuts that scabbed hieroglyphics into my burr cut.

August 23, 1955: **Pedaled to a dirty dip.**

Though I lived in the Land of 10,000 lakes, I didn't often swim. Neither my nor friends' families owned a cabin on the city's many surrounding lakes. (Well, Grandpa B did, but Haenke Lake was not conducive to swimming.) And I had neither permission nor nerve enough to go near abandoned mine pits that had filled with water that, only a few steps from shore, was hundreds of feet deep.

Forty-four-acre Silver Lake, in the middle of town, was an easy bike ride away and had a sandy beach and a cement-block change house. But it was often closed.

From 1910 to 1929, white pine logs had clogged the formerly pristine water to the point it was sometimes possible to walk across. Several young ersatz Jesuses of the day did, except for one kid who slipped between and beneath the logs and didn't rise again. The timber fed the world's largest white-pine saw mill, which disgorged up to a million boards a day from Silver Lake's southeast shore. Residue from the operation sank to the shallow lake's bottom and rotted to muck. Also, discharge from the world's largest municipal steam-heating plant, which stood on the former mill site, helped dye the water yellow.

The crud count from the submerged compost and effluent regularly rose to levels that forced health officials to close the beach for lengthy periods. And during the entire summer of 1951, after a warning that the polluted waters were potential petri dishes for the polio virus, no one swam in Silver Lake.

But none of that bothered me today, with temperatures in the high eighties. I accepted Silver Lake for what it was—available—and waded into the ooze and urine-colored water.

September 12, 1955: **Life as I've known it ends.**

I wasn't surprised by the doctor's diagnosis. But his prescription was devastating.

From first through fourth grades, my teachers had seated us alphabetically. Because my last name begins with "B," I usually sat in the first row, second desk back. But Miss Soper, my fifth grade teacher, arranged us seemingly randomly and placed me in the last seat in the last row. From there, I couldn't make out what she wrote on the blackboard. It was a blur.

So Mom took me to the offices of "MacDonald-Sipola Optometrists." Dr. MacDonald confirmed my nearsightedness, ordered corrective lenses and frames, and told Mom, "Don't let Gary read anything more than what's required at school. By the time he goes to college, he'll be able to throw away his glasses."

Mom complied and enforced, and my most-consistent source of pleasure—voracious reading—abruptly ended. Until I went to college. Wearing my glasses.

September 19, 1955: **Finally faced the music.**

After a year of my persistent pleading, Mom and Dad relented and said they'd pay for music lessons. Though television's piano-playing Liberace had been my main motivation and inspiration, I was determined to squeeze my music out of the Iron Range's national instrument, the accordion.

I entered a closet-size back room at Beddow's Music, at the west end of Chestnut Street, with instructor Gus Josephson for my first lesson. He plucked a small, worn twelve-bass loaner off a shelf, strapped it on me, then eased into his huge 120-bass model. He closed the door and lit up a Pall Mall as I located middle C.

During smokey half-hour weekly sessions over the next seven years, Gus—who played in a popular bar trio, The Smoothies—turned me into a virtuoso accordionist. Just as rock-and-roll guitar bands took over. So when I went away to college, I left my 120-bass Hohner behind and never played an accordion again.

September 28, 1955: **Dad didn't duck the question.**

We hunted and ate rabbits, partridge, and deer, but not ducks. As water-fowl season once again approached, I thought to ask Dad why we didn't.

"They're not grain-fed here, like other places," he explained. "So why waste time goin' after somethin' that's gonna taste like a swamp."

October 15, 1955: **Received a kickback.**

For a year and a half, I'd been occasionally allowed to plink tiny pieces of lead from Dad's .22 rifle into inanimate targets such as pine cones and tin cans atop fence posts.

Today, while exiting a partridge-hunting session with Grandpa B, he decided it was time for me to graduate from stills to live action. He handed me his 20-gauge shotgun, pointed to a flock of snowbirds pecking in the middle of a two-track, and gave me the go-ahead to blast a shot at them. He also cautioned me to cushion the gun's recoil by snugging the butt against my shoulder.

Apprehensive, I instead moved the stock away from my body as I pulled the trigger.

I didn't see the wad of BBs spray dust ten yards in front of the juncos, sending every bird into flight undamaged. The gun's "kick," however, had slammed into my shoulder so hard it had nearly knocked me over backward, welling my eyes with tears of pain and embarrassment and bruising my body and pride.

October 18, 1955: **Robin Hood reminds me to dial.**

A Bell Telephone representative visited our classroom and instructed us how to use the new dial phones that would soon be installed in our homes. Virginia's prefix was SHerwood, as in Sherwood Forest, he explained. Grandma and Grandpa B's Mt. Iron exchange was REpublic. I quickly memorized our new dial-up, SH1-3594, but also never forgot our former, "Number please," operator-activated, party-line connection, 2465J.

November 29, 1955: **Forgave God.**

My five-year-old cousin, Darlene Barfknecht, died of leukemia today. I was upset God hurt my Uncle Wilson, Aunt Mary, and cousin Wilson, Jr., so deeply.

But not long after, I learned that Aunt Mary was pregnant. And I thought, "Okay, God realized he made a mistake and is now making up for it."

Range-Speak

DURING JUST TEN YEARS around the turn of the twentieth century, near-guaranteed employment plus the promise of political and social freedom drew nearly 55,000 immigrants from more than forty ethnic backgrounds to the Mesabi. Most arrived with little more than their language.

Communication in the mines was critical, however, so the newcomers committed to rapidly learning English. In the process, each ethnic group fractured, salted, and otherwise altered their adopted tongue. The synergistic exercise developed a distinctive dialect that approached its own language.

The Range brogue stands out even among other Minnesotans, who themselves are recognizably accented. And outside the state, we were sometimes quizzed, "What country are you from?"

Our answer: "Da Raynche."

Encryption

Rangers
pronounce *th*'s **followed by vowels as** *d*'s.

"This, that, there" and "them," for examples, are *dis, dat, dare,* and *dem.* "The" is *da;* "other" / *udder.*

Linguists describe the substitution as replacing dental fricatives with alveolar stops. (And they say Rangers talk funny?)

pronounce *th*'s **followed by an** *r* **or at the end of words as** *t*'s.

"With" is *wit* (older Finnish Rangers said *wheat;*) "through" / *true;* "three"/ *tree.*

Combining both *th* alterations, "I think I saw three other things over there with them" is *I tink I saw tree udder tings over dare wheat dem.* "Through thick and thin" / *True tick and tin.*

replace *of* and *to* with *uh.*

"Most of" / *mostuh;* "have to" / *haftuh;* "in back of" / *in backuh;* "to the" / *tuhda.*

"Most of us had to ride in the pickup bed to the Fourth of July parade," translates to *Mostuh us hadduh ride in da back of da pickup tuhda Fortuh July parade.*

pronounce *oys* as *oyce* and *ors* as *orce.*

"Boys" is *boyce;* "toys" / *toyce;* "noise" / *noyce;* "doors" / *dorce*

"Those boys made a lot of noise slamming them doors." / *Dose boyce made a lottuh noyce slammin' dem dorce.*

economize letters.

For examples, "you" is *ya;* "your" or "you're" / *yer.* And *g's* are dropped from "*ing*" words: "Getting" / *getten;* "going"/ *goin';* "thinking" / *tinken.*

combine words into hybrids.

"I'm going to" is *I'm'n'a;* "in there" / *innair;* "out of" or "ought to" / *ahtta;*

economize phrasing.

"I'm going to go to the show" reduces to *I'm'n'a go show* or just *goin show* . "Do you want to go with me" is *Wanna go wit?*

end sentences with *eh*, for emphasis or to seek an affirmative response.

So ya caught yer limit, eh! So dat's a pretty good tomato, eh?

extraneously end some sentences with *then*.

So how's yer car been runnin' then? (Note: in this usage, "then" is not pronounced *den.* Go figure.)

end conversational segments with *you bet.*

It's all-purpose and can mean anything from "you're welcome" (*Tanks for da ride. / You bet.*) to "I agree" (*Boy, it snowed like hell yesterday. / You bet.*) to an enthusiastic "yeah" (*Wanna go wit tuhda hockey game? / You bet!*)

Decryption

about: Rangers pronounce this word more distinctly than anyone else. They form their mouths as though voicing a purse-lipped *oh*, then exhale a fusion of *a boat* and the Canadian *a boot* punctuated with a separate, staccato, third-syllable *t*.

biffy: originally meant outhouse, then evolved to mean any bathroom.

I gottuh go tuhda biffy.

boatadem: both of them.

Boy, you can't tell boatadem twins apart.

boofay: smorgsasbord.

Boy, ya sure get a lottuh bang for da buck at dat new Sveden House boofay.

boughten: anything you don't make yourself.

Da school cafeteria serves boughten bread.

chello: jello.

All dat wikkles is not chello.

chump: jump

Yer battree need a chump?

crotch: garage.

I carpeted my crotch wit brand-new pieces of used-up conveyor belt from da mine.

da cities: the twin cities, Minneapolis and St. Paul.

Boy, it takes haffuh day to drive tuhda cities.

Daloot: Duluth.

He hadduh drive tuhda Daloot to get dat special part.

eeder / needer: either / neither

I tink eeder one of dem bolts will fit. Nah, needer does.

enunder: underneath.

Crawl enunder da Chev and drain da oil.

er: her, but mostly applied to inanimate objects, particularly engines.

Start er up and let er run.

goofy: anything new, different, unusual.

Boy, dat Elvis sure got goofy hair, eh.

gooms: the flesh that anchors, or used to, your teeth.

Grandma smacks her gooms after she takes out her falsies.

got my ears lowered: got a hair cut.

hold yer noot, I held er for you: don't rush me. This isn't a Rangism, just something Grandpa B used to say.

jask: did you ask?

Jask who dat was he was wit?

jeet: did you eat?

Jeet any of dat hot dish wit da wild rice?

juhgo: did you go?
Juhgo huntin' wit your brudder?

kits: children.
Dey got tree kits, wit anudder on da way.

nuttin: nothing.
I ain't got nuttin tuh do.

pank: compress, particularly snow.
We panked a pat true da woods wit our boots.

pert near: almost.
I pert near busted true da tin ice.

pry: probably.
I'll pry go show wit da boyce dis Friday.

puntle: bundle.
Move dat puntle of boards over dare.

rasslin or rassler: wrestling or wrestler.
Boy, for a Minnesota farmboy, dat champ Verne Gagne is a heckuva rassler, eh."

rekalar: regular.
For a rich bastard, he seems to be a pretty rekalar guy, eh?

sauna: Rangers do not, I repeat do not say *sawna*. They pronounce the *ou* as in *ouch*, up-inflecting with a tease of enthusiasm; trail off with *ow*, as in *sow* (the pig), with a trace of disappointment; then down-inflect the *na* with a hint of determination.

sumpin: something.
Boy dem clowns on da city council are really sumpin, eh.

tan que: thank you. Although most Rangers just say, *tanks*.

<u>January 14, 1956</u>: **Limb lost to liquor.**

As Dad and I left Grande Hardware, I stared down the sidewalk at a schoolmate's father. The bottom half of his right pant leg was folded up and pinned near his waist, and he swung-walked on his left leg with the help of wood crutches. I asked Dad if the man had been injured at the mine.

"Nah," Dad replied with a hint of disdain, "he passed out drunk walking home after the bars closed. By the time somebody found him, his leg was froze so bad they had to cut it off."

February 16, 1956: **Didn't like sending Dad out into the cold.**

I insisted on staying up past my bedtime to say goodbye to Dad as he left to work a midnight shift. I had pulled on flannel pj's, and Dad had layered himself in cotton and wool to spend the fifteen-below-zero night pulling levers and pushing pedals in the cab of a huge power shovel. Dad disappeared into the black cold, and I felt uncomfortable crawling under my warm, heavy covers.

February 26, 1956: **Tommy's play was unconscious.**

Tommy Matkovich jumped into our street-hockey game on his way to a friend's house down the block. However, he was wearing only leather-soled street shoes for the short walk. We laughed as he slipped, slid, and fell on our snow-covered, car-compacted road rink.

Suddenly, Tommy's feet shot skyward, pivoting the back of his head to an audible street slam. He moaned and his eyes rolled back into his head. My good friend Charlie Stupca and I picked him up, wrapped his limp arms around our shoulders, dragged him to his house, and knocked.

Mrs. Matkovich slapped both hands against her mouth and gasped at our presentation of her semiconscious son. But she quickly regained her composure, took Tommy inside, and Charlie and I returned to the game. Next day, Tommy showed up at school, seemingly no worse for the experience.

March 15, 1956: **Got a well-deserved birthday surprise.**

My grade-school marks were good, except in one subject: Conduct. My report cards consistently included comments like, "Excellent student, but talks too much."

In fifth grade, I discovered a new diversion. I tipped backwards and attempted to balance on my chair's back legs. When I again crashed after Miss Soper's final warning, she sighed, "If you insist on acting like a five-year-old, you're going to sit like one." Whereupon she accompanied me to the kindergarten classroom and directed me to carry one of their smaller chairs back to my desk. When I continued my failed balancing acts, she moved my desk and the kindergarten chair next to hers facing the class.

Then today, on my birthday, she bent me over her lap and administered eleven mock strokes to my behind with a real wood paddle. On it was printed, "The board of education for the seat of all learning."

April 15, 1956: **Sister suffered a callous Christian.**

As we drove home from church, Kathy began sobbing. Mom coaxed out why. Kathy's Sunday school teacher had told her that her twin sister, Carol, who had died two days after birth, was not in heaven because she had not been baptized. Mom assured Kathy that Carol was in heaven and that her Sunday school teacher might not be going there for saying something so cruel.

May 12, 1956: **Familiarity breeds predictability.**

Our '56 Chevrolet 210 sedan, though basic, did come equipped with a new standard feature, electric turn signals. Which Dad didn't use. Probably just habit that some subtle retraining would break, I figured. So just before a left turn on the short trip home from town, I encouraged him to flick down the black-knobbed lever that stuck out from the steering column.

"Don't need to," he responded in all sincerity. "Everybody knows where I'm going."

The author's family's new 1956 Chevrolet. (Author collection)

June 23, 1956: **Risked arrest by bastardizing baseball.**

I swiped a fistful of Mom's wood peg clothespins out of the cloth bag hanging from our outdoor lines and pedaled to Charlie Stupca's house. Meanwhile, Charlie shaped one end of a wood crate slat into a handle, creating a cricket-type bat. We then played our two-man street distortion of the national pastime.

Whoever was "up" stood on the sidewalk, and the opposing pitcher hurled a clothespin from the middle of the street. When the batter connected, the distance the clothespin went on the fly before landing determined scoring, which ranged from a feeble, spinning-tap double play to a rocket, across-the-street home run.

A sidewalk segment fronting Charlie's house served as our usual batter's box. Today, however, strong winds forced us to reverse our field and bat from across the street. Unfortunately, left-field home-run territory then included the mean-old-lady's house next door to Charlie's. Sure enough, as had happened before, Charlie whacked a clothespin off her front window. Not only was it a homer but also game over, because, as had happened before, she burst out the front door shrieking threats to call the police.

June 26, 1956: **Dad kicked my butt.**

Adults rarely intervened in the fist fights that sometimes interrupted our play. When they did, they usually just yelled, "Break it up," and we did.

Not Dad. The former Golden Gloves boxer sometimes stepped in with two pairs of fighter's gloves, made us combatants put them on "so you don't hurt each other," then resume while he refereed. But by the time we laced up the padded leather mitts, we didn't feel like fighting any more. Dad made us finish anyway, meaning until somebody got the wind knocked out of them, said, "I give," or suffered a bloody nose. Dad once even tried to make Reenie and Kathy settle an intense argument the same way. But he relented when they cried, then laughed as he struggled to secure the adult gloves to their tiny hands.

Today's playground scrap between Larry Hunsinger and me was more intense than usual. We grappled and punched so hard for so long that Mrs. Routsi—her "break it up" shouts ignored—crossed the street and physically separated us. But as she re-entered her house, Larry and I went back at it.

Suddenly, Dad loomed large, but without boxing gloves. He levitated me by my shirt collar with one hand, and while dangling me home, delivered a token kick to my rump with the side of his foot while admonishing, "When an adult breaks you up, you stop!"

It was and would be the only time Dad ever laid a hand . . . or foot . . . on me.

July 10, 1956: **Dad relocated a neighborhood pest.**

"What's that for?" I asked, observing Dad complete construction of what appeared to be just a crude wood box.

Dad said he was going to catch a rogue skunk that had been rooting through neighborhood garbage and gardens. He then showed me how his trap worked. The compartment was big enough to accommodate the skunk, he explained, without allowing it to raise its tail and spray. A piece of monofilament suspended a hinged door open inward at the back of the box and was connected to a rudimentary release mechanism at the front. Dad placed a piece of bacon on that "trigger." When the skunk entered the box and took the bait, he explained, the door would drop closed behind it.

Next morning, the door was shut and the box was heavy. Dad lifted it into our car trunk and said, "C'mon."

I figured we were going to release the animal somewhere into the surrounding woods but wondered how Dad would do it without us getting sprayed. We parked off Highway 7, and Dad handed me a shovel to shoulder as he lugged the trapped skunk over a well-worn path along the shore of Four Mile Lake. About a quarter mile in, Dad pulled a cord from his pocket, tied one end to the box, and heaved it out into the lake. As it sank, Dad dug a hole several yards off the trail. He then grabbed the cord, pulled the execution chamber back to shore, dumped the carcass into the grave, covered it, and we returned home.

July 18, 1956: **Charlie invented jarts.**

I pedaled up to Charlie's garage as he and his cousin Dennis O'Leary arrived on foot. On their walk from Dennis's house, they had crossed a gun club's grounds on the shore of Silver Lake. Littering the grass were dozens of shells ejected from shotguns that had loosed buckshot at clay pigeons flung out over the water the evening before.

Charlie and Dennis picked up several empty casings plus pocketfuls of feathers shed by ducks that waddled around the area. At Charlie's direction in his garage, we inserted a spray of feathers quill-side down into the open end of each of the spent shells then folded over and pinched together the cardboard cylinders' thin, fluted tops. When done, we sank an empty soup can into the lawn so that the open end was at ground level.

We then stepped back twenty feet and took turns arcing our feathered projectiles underhand at the can, scoring a point for each direct potshot. The carefully engineered feather placement ensured aerodynamic stability and accuracy, and the shells' heavier, brass-capped bottoms caused them to consistently land right side down.

July 29, 1956: **Mom blasphemed.**

On our way home from church, Mom sputtered about her adult Sunday school lay teacher, Mr. Sturdy. He had said that while driving to First Covenant he had seen a boy carrying a fishing pole. "He sure wasn't on his way to services," stern Sturdy had judged.

"Maybe he went to early Mass," Mom said she had let slip.

"They're going to burn in hell, too," Sturdy snapped.

Mom's position was consistent; Sturdy's comeback was surprisingly frank. Though Mom had long attended First Covenant, she had not officially joined because she did not subscribe to all of their tenets. And though our church was philosophically anti-Catholic, an outburst like Sturdy's was unusual, even within First Covenant's sanctuary. First Covenant struggled to maintain a membership of 100. Queen City Catholics supported three churches plus a parochial school. Though not biblical, the name "Custer" probably resonated with our church members, especially business owners.

I didn't understand anti-Catholicism. My three best friends were Catholic, and the only differences I had noted between their religion and mine was that they couldn't eat meat on Friday, and before Easter they showed up at school with black smudges on their foreheads. Didn't seem like they'd go to hell for that. Also puzzling, I had often heard our church members say that children were gifts from God. If Catholics were not favored by God, why did He bestow so many such gifts upon them?

August 12,1956: **Feasted on fish and chips.**

Dad and I returned from one of our few fishing trips to Lake Vermilion with enough walleyes for supper. And Mom prepared them my favorite way—coated with crushed Old Dutch potato chips then baked.

August 22, 1956: **Lost a found baseball.**

We had literally knocked the covers off every baseball used in our sporadic neighborhood games. So Dad sewed the leather back onto mine with a sailmaker's needle and black fishing line. Not only did we have a ball that might last the remainder of the season, but we could also see its seams like big leaguers.

Dad also suggested a way to get a free, near-new replacement. The Senior A Mesabi League played at Ewens Field, on the north side of town. Several times each game, foul balls arced out of the stadium and landed in a no-mans land behind the roofed home-plate seats and Sixth Avenue. Dad said that if I was there when it happened, I could take the ball.

I decided to try and didn't have to wait long for the first ball to drop out of the sky just yards away. I grabbed it, then felt a sharp tap on my shoulder. I turned and faced Lester Lane, one of the town's toughest kids. The league had hired him to retrieve the foul balls. I handed Lester my pickup and biked home without balls.

September 4, 1956: **Entered my first new classroom in my last year.**

My austere dark-brick James Madison elementary school was built in 1926 and looked it. My first four teachers had taught there since the school opened and looked it. All four also retired immediately after I occupied their classrooms, but I'm sure that was coincidental.

To accommodate the influx of baby boomers, a contemporary blond-brick south wing had been constructed in 1954, and a similar north wing had just opened.

I had learned in the original classrooms from kindergarten through fifth grade. But during this, my final year at Madison, I got assigned to a room in the south addition. And though only two years old, it had already been refurbished, after a custodian using a blow torch to thaw pipes had accidentally started a fire that seriously damaged the room.

September 14, 1956: **Native American allusion is illusion.**

In 1952, new owners had renamed Bailey Lumber Yard, "Pohaki Lumber Company." I liked the name, and figured they had honored a historic Native American. The company's new logo even resembled the Indian on old nickels.

I finally thought to ask classmate Tom Kintner to pass my compliments along to his father, one of Pohaki's owners. Tom said he would, but added that his dad and two partners had actually formed the native-sounding moniker as an acronym from their last names—POgorelce, HAhne and KIntner.

October 13, 1956: **Choked down another pasty.**

Pasties (pass'-tees), a cuisine introduced to the Mesabi by Cornish immigrants, gained such pervasive popularity that outsiders called it "the national food of the Range."

I, however, couldn't stand the stuff. According to everyone else, Grandma B's version of the mixture of inexpensive chopped beef pieces, sliced root vegetables (turnip, rutabaga, carrots), diced potatoes, chopped onions, and seasonings, wrapped in dough and baked was to die for. And I did appreciate that her meat pies were convenient, hearty at-work lunches for Grandpa.

But as an underdeveloped kid with an overdeveloped gag reflex, I had a hard time downing rutabaga and sometimes-gristly meat chunks. So again tonight, to render my pasty edible and not offend Grandma, I doused the "delicacy" with ketchup.

November 9, 1956: **New classmate is more than a little unpleasant.**

Mr. Christensen, our teacher and principal, informed us that a new student would join our class on Monday. Her name was Marilyn, he said, then prepared us that she was a little different. Marilyn, as we found out, was what is now termed a "proportionate dwarf," what we then called a midget. Though about half the normal size, she was perfectly proportioned. But she also sounded like she had inhaled helium.

We sixth-graders had absorbed enough Range mores to inherently, initially accept Marilyn. As long as she didn't complain about what life had dealt her, she'd fit in. And she didn't complain. However, Marilyn exhibited another abnormality we couldn't tolerate. She was an obnoxious, self-centered, selfish spoiled brat who alienated everyone.

I didn't know where Marilyn had come from. I didn't know where she lived. I didn't know if she had a family. I never saw her outside of school. And a few months later, for reasons not revealed to us, she disappeared.

November 17, 1956 : **Got rid of my recessive jeans.**

One set of my dungarees had transitioned from "growinta" to outgrown, so Mom took me to Ketolas Department store for a replacement pair. As always, she selected a size not clown large but that I could wear for a school year, maybe two.

The denim was near board-stiff but, being oversize, the stovepipe-shaped legs were easy to step into. And, rolling up their bottoms added a fashion accent by revealing the red-plaid flannel lining.

At home I cinched up my new Wranglers with a new hand-me-down belt from Dad. He had punched additional holes in the leather strap, and when I buckled it, the surplus tail flopped down to the side. As my waistline gradually expanded over the years, I moved down the line of holes. But the belt disintegrated before I reached a factory setting.

December 27, 1956: **Lovely weather for a sleigh ride together.**

At our former farm, now owned by Dad's brother, Grandpa Stoltz braided the team of work horses' tails, groomed their manes, cinched leather harnesses, and attached brass bells and red ribbons. Next he covered the worn planks of a working sleigh bed with a thick layer of clean hay and stacked on a pile of wool, army-surplus blankets.

He hitched up the horses then headed out on a route in and around Virginia to pick up his eleven area grandchildren in front of their houses. We were last.

Bells on braided tails rang and made our spirits bright as we then skidded from our house over car-compacted snow on Eighteenth Street to the former airport. The sleigh set tracks across that snow-covered field, then crushed brush out to Highway 7 and my favorite part of the ride. There, we first dove, seemingly almost straight down, into a deep ditch. Grandpa then furiously slapped reins and yelled, "Giddap, giddap, giddap," as the horses jerked us also seemingly straight up the other side.

After grating across the plowed-bare, paved highway, we repeated the plunge and rise, this time onto a wide, level trail into an area someone sometime before had named Sun Valley. Those of us who lived life on the edge of the sleigh sometimes got pitched off during the ditching. At other times, we deliberately did cannonball dives off our wood platform into deep drifts and banks, then hopped onto the sleigh's rear runners and rode awhile before hoisting ourselves back up topside.

To equalize ride time, on the return Grandpa reversed the pickup route, dropping my sisters and me off last.

Family sleigh ride. (Author collection)

Complicated First Kill

On a near-seventy-degree October Sunday, Dad and I set out on an afternoon of partridge hunting. Well, for Dad it was hunting. I had yet to shoot anything that moved. And chances of hitting a partridge with a pea-sized .22 bullet would be greater than a literal long shot. Naturally camouflaged, the chicken-size fowl blended into ground cover until we nearly stepped on them. Then they exploded into the air, their two-foot wingspans generating startling sonic mini-booms as they near-instantly accelerated to a forty-miles-per-hour twisting, weaving vanishment.

As I moved through the forest, a stationary red squirrel scolded me from a pine branch directly overhead. Anxious and curious to find out what it was like to kill, I aimed my .22 at the bushy-tailed chatterer and squeezed the trigger. The squirrel dropped off the branch onto a bed of needles and leaves just inches from my boot tips.

My marksmanship surprised me. I had sent the lead through the small animal's chest, and the tiny hole discharged a bright-red trickle as the squirrel, eyes closed and oversized tail twitching, bit at the air a few final times. The image disturbed me, but only until I decided to commemorate the moment by stuffing and mounting my victim, like the lifelike dead animals I had seen displayed in Mac's bar. I carried the squirrel by its tail to our Chev and placed it in the trunk next to two partridge dad had bagged. At home, I shrouded the furry bundle in a rag, and placed it in our basement chest freezer.

Next day, I checked out an illustrated, step-by-step, how-to taxidermy book from the our city library. Over the following four nights, I studied the "Small Animal" chapter, then on Friday pulled the carcass out of the freezer to thaw.

And on Saturday morning I set out to bring the animal back to artificial life. Dad had carpooled to work, and Mom had driven our Chev to shop at the Red Owl super market.

Step one, skinning, was pretty easy. Except for some intricate surgery required at the head and tail areas, I'd performed the operation many times before while helping Dad or Grandpa field-dress rabbits for dinner. At step two, however, I recognized I did not possess the materials, finesse, or inclination to create an artificial skull, as recommended.

So I went with the book's only other option, use the original skull. The first step in that process was to boil the brains out of and residual flesh off the rodent's cranium. So I plopped the skinless head into Mom's heavy iron soup pot, added water, set it on a front burner of our electric stove, and cranked the dial to "High."

Soon after, Mom returned and, while setting down grocery bags, groaned, "Gawwwd, what's that smell?!" Before I could respond, she peered into the pot just as the tiny bone face roiled up and grinned.

I expected a lecture followed by a grounding. But whether stunned near-silent or maybe suppressing shocked laughter, Mom just headed back out to the car for more bags while directing, "Get rid of that thing before I get back."

I was relieved Mom had ended the project because, long before submerging the squirrel skull, I had sensed I was in way over my head.

I discarded the squirrel's remains, except for its bushy foot-long tail, which I placed atop my red plastic radio. Over the next couple of weeks, the appendage rigor mortised, with only faint odor, into a question-mark shape. I then used it to sneak up behind my sisters and tickle their ears or necks, whereupon shortly thereafter, my stiff, fuzzy trophy mysteriously disappeared.

Yuletide Sacrifices

DAD DECLARED MY FIRST ANNUAL day of holiday hell on the eve of my sixth-grade Christmas break. He lowered the *Mesabi Daily News*; directed, "Gar, get us a Christmas tree tomorrow;" and returned to reading.

"Okay," I grunted while focusing on the assembly of a plastic Hellcat model airplane. I figured the assignment wouldn't be too demanding, even for a short, scrawny eleven-year-old. After all, thousands of nature-grown evergreens spread out not far from our back door. Plus, the two previous seasons I had "helped" Dad cut our family's wild and free holiday trees. And he'd made it look easy.

So after Dad left for work the next morning, I spit on a carborundum stone and honed the blades of our double-bit ax. I then layered myself in winter wear and set out with the ax and a small bucksaw two miles—south down railroad tracks, west along Southern Drive, across Highway 7, then on a trail through Sun Valley swampland to a stand of mixed evergreens.

There, following Dad's example, I bushwhacked through snow and brush to a cluster of balsam firs. En route I passed up several attractive spruces, because Dad had said that even in a sugar-water-filled stand, their needles rapidly dried and dropped like rain.

So, per Dad's past practice, I would select one of the durable balsams. But the best candidates in the crowd sprouted unobstructed from the tops of the tallest trees. Plus, heavy snow clung to and obscured those twenty- to twenty-five-foot high crowns. So to reveal and assess from below, I'd have to dislodge the white stuff by whacking the trunks with the the ax.

I picked out a promising specimen and pulled down my parka hood to get an unobstructed look at my home-run swing into the trunk. The balsam shuddered and, as I reflexively snapped my head up to watch, shed its mantle.

The cascading snow caked my glasses and packed into the interface between my coat and neck. With no effective way to clean and dry the lenses, I shoved the eyewear into my parka pocket.

After also scooping out the snow that had begun trickling down my back, I chopped a notch into the trunk on the side I had assessed clear enough for the tree to topple unobstructed. Next I sawed into the opposite side until I heard the satisfying crack of separating wood. I stepped away from a potential kickback as I hollered, "Timber." By the time my warning to no one echoed back, however, the tree had swayed a mere six feet to a leaning embrace with a neighbor. I tried to separate the couple but couldn't. So I moved to another candidate, dislodged and dodged its snowcap, and judged its upper reaches to be perfect. I then successfully felled it only to discover that my now-uncorrected myopia had blurred the top to phantom fullness.

Two more visually impaired, chance attempts may have violated the letter but, I rationalized, not the spirit of rule #1 on the Boy Scout *Totin' Chip* card I had earned: "I will not cut living trees needlessly."

The prolonged exercise temporarily exorcised my Christmas spirit. Exhausted, frustrated, wet, hungry, and stained with sticky pitch that had bled from the victims of my serial slashings, I ended my spree. I sawed the top six feet off a default downer and dragged it and my butt home. I let go of the tree near our back steps and shuffled to our garage, where I soaked a rag with gasoline and swabbed sap off my tools and hands. I then showered, washed down a grilled cheese sandwich with tomato soup, flopped onto the couch, and read *Classics Comics* until Dad arrived. Then, I expected, we'd secure my tree in our metal stand and place it next to our fireplace.

Shortly after 4:00, Dad pulled into the driveway, and I stepped out the door as he reached the supine balsam. When he raised it, my erratic preteen self-esteem flat-lined. The drag home across snow, asphalt, gravel, and railroad ties and cinders had rasped off the tree's slide-side needles. Dad scanned the bald strip and counseled, "You shoulduh left it by the highway."

"Then what?" I asked.

"We'd go get it now and bring it back in the car," he replied, up-intonating "car," suggesting that the answer should have been obvious. He then set his lunch pail inside and directed, "Let's go," insinuating resignation by down-intonating "go." I knew why we were leaving but didn't risk further inflections by asking where.

Dad threw the ax, saw, and an army-surplus blanket into our Chev's trunk. As the sun set over an Oliver Mining Company dump and into their pit four miles west, we drove north through, then out of town. Not far past the city limits, Dad turned onto a two-track that skirted the base of an out-of-service dump at his workplace, M.A. Hanna's Enterprise mine. A decade before, the company had stabilized and beautified the high, expansive ridge by planting thousands of pine seedlings. Some had grown to ideal Christmas-tree height and shape.

A quarter mile from the highway we stopped and switchbacked on foot up the steep slope. Then, in the twilight, Dad swiftly removed a near-perfect Norway pine, with a straight, slender, red-barked trunk; thick, upswept branches; and well-formed crown. Minutes later we wrapped the tree in the blanket and placed it in the Chev's trunk. We then mostly closed and loosely tied down the lid, with the shrouded tree's tip sticking out, and took unlit back roads home. (In another time, or perhaps more so another place, I suppose Dad's trespassing and petty theft might have been considered unlawful. To Rangers then, however, the tree would have been considered a non-contractual fringe benefit.)

After dinner dishwashing, we strung lights, hung ornaments, and draped tinsel—most saved from last year—on the long-needled pine. Mom's ceremonial step-stool tree-topping with an aluminum star brought a positive, but only temporary end to my ordeal.

Turned out Dad had issued a standing directive. So for the next six Christmases, I removed a tree from Sun Valley. And the first two of those seasons, after Dad's inspection, we again made surreptitious dump runs. But my unnatural-selection technique did evolve to the point that, at ages sixteen and seventeen, I drove to the Valley myself and downed a balsam I had previously inspected, selected and marked during warm weather. I then readied the lush upper six feet in a stand in our living room corner, knowing Dad no longer needed to validate.

Even then, I indulged the spirit of Christmas frugal only because I had to. I couldn't wait to forsake it. After leaving home, I didn't get a tree until married and then reluctantly until I had children. And I *purchased* every one of the evergreens. But—Norman Rockwell and Currier & Ives be damned—never at a U-cut-it-yourself farm.

January 6, 1957: **Waited for Elvis.**

I was entertained more by the concept that there could *be* an Elvis Presley than his music. So I had watched his first two appearances on the *Ed Sullivan Show* mostly with curiosity.

98

Tonight I was ambivalent. In our Central Time Zone, Sullivan ran from 7:00 to 8:00 p.m. Lights-out at the rink was 9:00, which meant limiting my Sunday night hockey to barely an hour. But Presley's appearance was billed as his last on Sullivan, so I decided to watch.

I finished homework while an impressionist, a ventriloquist, and a new comedienne, Carol Burnett, performed between Elvis sets. Then, as Elvis closed his eyes and dropped his chin to chest during the last notes of his finale, "Peace in the Valley," I dashed out the door with skates and stick.

January 7, 1957: **A hit worthy of the mob.**

Following lunch the first day after Christmas break, our sixth-grade teacher, Mr. Roy, unexpectedly and inexplicably appointed me our class's first "president." He then informed me that I would serve only a one-afternoon term and that my sole duty was to inform him of anyone who talked when he left the room. If I didn't, he warned, I would spend indeterminate time writing after-school essays.

He then stepped out and didn't return until dismissal. I reluctantly compiled a talker list with repeat-violation checkmarks and handed the rap sheet to Mr. Roy. He congratulated me on a job well done and said he knew the list was accurate because he had been monitoring via the school's two-way p.a. system. Next morning he sentenced the three top conversationalists—Dave, Donald, and Bobby—to three days each of after-school essay writing.

When paroled, they exacted retribution. Dave recruited the cutest girl in our class to lure me to an after-school rendezvous. To appear oh-so cool, I unzipped my coat nearly to my waist and Elvis-flipped up the collar. I then stepped outside and moved to the slick, panked snow in front of her. I pressed my boots tightly together to avoid self-consciously shuffling my feet, then stared at them while swinging a folder full of homework papers.

From around the corner close behind, the avengers struck. Donald yanked back my upturned collar and jammed in a handful of snow. Simultaneously, Bobby swatted my folder, sending papers fluttering to a looseleaf, uncollated landing. Dave then slide-slammed his boot into my conjoined feet, knocking them out from under me and levitating me temporarily parallel with the paper pile before dropping into it.

The following Monday, Mr. Roy appointed Dave as afternoon president. Dave didn't take down names, however, so wrote after-school essays the rest of the week.

Years later I found out that we all had been guinea pigs in an experiment Roy had concocted in pursuit of an advanced degree.

January 15, 1957: Received cold-cash payments.

Delivering seventy-two copies of the Sunday *Minneapolis Tribune* in the relentless sub-zero January temperatures was quicker and more comfortable than getting paid for it. At 5:00 a.m., I dressed defensively, generated heat with non-stop movement, and at 7:00 crawled back under the covers until Mom rousted me for church a couple of hours later.

But after school today, I began another miserable week of collecting the thirty-five cents per paper, of which I netted a nickel. In negative-five-degree weather, I stepped up to each subscriber's door, knocked while yelling "collect," then waited for someone to answer. Most customers invited me in, which was a mixed blessing. The welcome warmth also instantly frosted my glasses. The coating usually melted by the time I stepped back outside, but the resulting thin layer of water then froze, causing artificial astigmatisms.

A few inconsiderates yelled, "Just a minute," and I hugged myself to stay warm while, judging from the elapsed time, they searched couch cushions for coins. Others opened their doors just wide enough to quickly hand me payment then re-

closed while I removed my mitts and ripped off their tiny, perforated, dated receipt stub.

On the other hand, a few generous readers prepaid a month at a time. And as always, at my last call, Mrs. Crogness gave me a warm cookie.

February 10, 1957: First concert fell on suppressed ears.

The author rehearsing for a church concert. (Author collection)

Mom decided that after a year and a half of accordion lessons I should play in public. So she booked a gig at church. I performed a flawless rendition of "Whispering Hope" to close evening services. But since displays of enthusiasm about anything, even God, were deemed inappropriate, I was not rewarded with applause, just solemn nods.

February 16, 1957: **Got a rise out of Dad.**

Dad maintained and repaired our cars, sometimes disassembling their engines to original components just to inspect, restore or replace, then reassemble. As I approached age twelve, he determined it was time for me to participate and "invited" me to join him in our unheated garage. As he disappeared under our '56 Chev to perform some mysterious operation, he informed me that my job was—like a surgeon's nurse—to shine a light from above and hand him instruments.

I did not perform well or with enthusiasm. I had no idea, for instance, what a three-quarter-inch socket on a half-inch drive was, so Dad growled, wiggled out, and handed it to himself. The work light I was supposed to focus wandered with my mind. And, while Dad stayed warm working, I was freezing my tools off.

My disinterested discomfort evidently showed, because Dad barked, "Pay attention. Some day you're gonna haftuh do this yourself."

I rarely talked back to Dad but let slip, "No, I'm not. I'm going to make enough money to pay someone else to do it."

In an equally rare display of emotion, Dad involuntarily rose and smacked his head. Fortunately, neither of us said anything further. Unfortunately, he didn't fire me.

March 15, 1957: **Received a rare gift.**

While I slept snugly through the night preceding my twelfth birthday, winds gusting up to sixty miles per hour whipped more than a foot of falling snow into white dunes up to ten feet high across the Range. In the morning, Virginia radio station WHLB issued a surprising announcement: school had been called off.

Surprising, because in my seven winters of education—each of which had included several feet of staying snowfall sometimes blown by blizzards—until this morning, school had never been cancelled.

May 31, 1957: **Caught an "ish."**

While trolling for walleyes on Lake Vermilion, my minnow took a sudden, tremendous hit. My metal rod whipped into horseshoe shape, and the open-face reel spun as I let whatever had struck head to the bottom. The fish didn't thrash like a walleye or northern but felt more like a surging log.

Burbot, lawyer, or ling. (Author collection)

I hauled up my catch, Dad netted it, and I recoiled as I removed the ugliest fish I had ever seen. Beady eyes glared at me from the front of its slick, eel-like body, which it tried wrapping around my arm. A pair of soft, rippling fins topped and bottomed its rear half, and a thick whisker dangled from its chin. Dad said the creature was a "lawyer" and, since it had swallowed the hook, added, "I'm gonna haftuh cut the damn line." He did, then also slit the lawyer's gills before throwing it back into the lake as lunch for circling gulls. Dad didn't say, but by his actions and the fish's appearance, I figured lawyers must be a "garbage" fish, probably too oily and strong-tasting to eat.

Decades later, however, I learned that anglers elsewhere purposely went after lawyers—also called burbot or ling—because they taste like lobster.

June 24, 1957: **Risked a pounding from Dad.**

Dad directed me to hold a six-foot steel fence post upright and steady while he sledge-hammered it into the ground. I trusted Dad implicitly, but this procedure gave me pause. For the first time, I almost refused his order. Dad sensed my apprehension approaching fear. "You know I worked on a railroad track gang for a couple of winters," he reassured.

So I hung on tightly and looked away, knowing that a flinch on my part might mean a broken arm. And it would be my fault. Dad arced the sixteen-pound sledge from behind his back, over his shoulder, and hit the pipe full force, dead center. Three more swings and he had driven the post far enough into the ground for me to release my white-knuckle grip.

July 6, 1957: **Handled some real crap.**

Dad hauled me, two shovels, and his homemade trailer a quarter mile from our house to a father-son outing at the city's sewage treatment plant. There, from one of the vegetation-covered knolls around the facility, we loaded a black-dirt-looking substance. I didn't ask but presumed was it the processed, decomposed waste eliminated by Queen City residents.

At home we fed the previously digested meals full-recycle to our backyard vegetable garden.

July 10, 1957: **Garden squashes were entertaining.**

One garden task Dad didn't have to remind me to carry out was to eradicate tomato worms. The exercise provided bursts of fun.

Though two to three inches long, the caterpillars weren't easy to spot directly. They hid on the undersides of our tomato plants' leaves and were the same color. But the larval pigs consumed so much, so fast, that the foliage they decimated betrayed their locations.

The pests were creepy ugly, with white V-shaped marks along their segmented sides and prominent black devil-like horns projecting from their butt ends. I didn't want to find out if they could sting, so I removed the worms with twigs, flicked them onto the sidewalk, and crushed them with my shoe, exploding a substance that looked like guacamole and smelled like tomatoes.

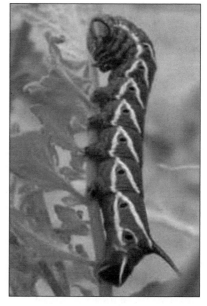

Tomato hornworm. (Author collection)

103

Dad's Good Deed Does Not Go Unpunished

July 14-20, 1957

OUR SCOUTMASTER AND OLDER TROOP members had traveled to the national Boy Scout Jamboree at Valley Forge, Pennsylvania. So Dad donated vacation time to spend what turned out to be a proverbial week in hell chaperoning a dozen of us younger scouts at Camp Wichingen, near Hibbing.

Our group was assigned to Long Walk, the campsite farthest from the mess hall/headquarters. We each shouldered a canvas packsack containing our clothing and toiletries and hiked the narrow, quarter-mile trail through the woods. Well, except for Lloyd. His parents struggled with two suitcases plus a packsack while Lloyd ambled unencumbered. At our grouping of canvas wall-tents set up over wood floors in a clearing, we rolled out our sleeping bags on cots and unpacked. My tent-mate tapped me on the shoulder and pointed across the opening to Lloyd pulling a backscratcher out of one of his suitcases. Minutes later, Lloyd threw a tantrum because he didn't have room to set out all his stuff. When his roommate refused to relinquish any of his space, Lloyd grabbed a hatchet and feigned a threat.

Whereupon, Dad confiscated the weapon and directed Lloyd to bunk with him. Whereupon, Lloyd threatened to stab Dad during the night. Whereupon, Dad promised to preclude by strapping Lloyd to his cot. Whereupon Lloyd calmed down and became Dad's docile cellmate for the duration.

Next morning, Lloyd self-inflicted more grief. At breakfast we were told that during meals we could take as much food as we wanted as long as we ate it all. Whereupon Lloyd stacked fifteen pancakes but ate only three. Whereupon at lunch, the leftovers were all Lloyd was served. Whereupon, it took him two more meals to ingest them all.

Next morning after breakfast, the camp director took Dad aside and whispered solemnly to him. Dad returned and relayed that a Virginia teenager, Bill Niemi, who lived near Charlie, had shotgunned his family, killing two. We were stunned. Nothing like that had ever happened in Virginia that we were aware of. Distraught thinking his occasional playmate, Tom, was one of the fatalities, Charlie sobbed while Dad consoled him. An hour later, we learned that Tom was alive but his mother and four-year-old sister were dead and his father wounded.

We all wanted to leave then, no one more so, I thought, than Dad, though he didn't let on. And for the next two peaceful days he was able to mostly stay in the background after handing us off to instructors at swimming, canoeing, archery, crafts, and other activities.

Then, on the fourth night, fierce winds, accompanied by lightning and driving rain, unexpectedly ripped through Wichingen. The camp director radioed Dad to march us through the turbulent blackness to shelter in the mess hall. Dad refused, judging the move too dangerous. He made the right call. As we tromped to breakfast in the wet morning calm, we climbed over or maneuvered around a half dozen trees that had been blown down across the trail.

We made it to the mess hall and sat down for a breakfast that preceded two final routine, uneventful days.

No Thrill on Blueberry Hill

August 5, 1957

W AY TOO EARLY IN THE MORNING, Dad rousted me for a family blueberry-picking expedition. As on previous such outings, he drove us to the end of some wilderness two-track, where we then bushwhacked through dew-covered brush to one of his secret patches. As always, insects seemed to grow in greater numbers than berries. And as always, Dad carried his Winchester .30-30 in case a black bear tried to compete for the same crop.

Soaked to the waist from the walk in, Mom, my sisters, and I then stooped, squatted and plopped for two hours, simultaneously swatting at mosquitoes and deer and horse flies while searching through thick greenery for blue fruit. Since most ripe berries were BB-size and -textured, any juicy find larger than the picker's little fingernail was announced with the shout, "I got one big as a damned grape!" then eaten.

Meanwhile, Dad attacked the bushes with his homemade picker. The wood, shoe-box-size contraption resembled a miniature version of the business end of the monstrous mining power shovels he operated. Gripping the wood handle atop the box, Dad repeatedly plunged the rake-toothed, open front end into the vegetation, scooped, and emptied into pails. Later at home, we kids spent another couple of hours dumping the buckets' contents onto newspapers and sorting through leaves, twigs, spiders, and unripened white and green nodules in search of actual blue berries.

But not until we had passed wood-tick inspection. Upstairs, Mom and my sisters stripped and searched each other, while Dad and I did same in the basement. Mom and Dad picked off crawling ticks and—since their titanium-hard exoskeletons couldn't be finger-, foot-, or even plier-crushed—swirled them down the toilet.

Those that had burrowed their blood-sucking heads under the skin required special removal. Convention proscribed plucking out the tiny invader with tweezers because its barbed proboscis would snap off and subcutaneously decay, possibly causing an infection. Convention prescribed applying a drop of kerosene or hot, extinguished match tip to the bug's bitty butt to force it to back out. Convention worked.

But researchers later determined that, just before the arachnid exited, the trauma caused it to simultaneously vomit, urinate and defecate.

August 10, 1957: **Brother, brother, pants on fire.**
Match guns were the most sophisticated and literally the hottest of my and a few contemporaries' home-made play weapons. By disassembling, custom notching, and reassembling a clip, coil-spring clothespin with a rubber band, we could simultaneously light and shoot stick matches. We competed for height or distance (ten to twenty feet), sometimes followed by the excitement of stomping out small grass fires we occasionally ignited. But we never aimed the mini-flamethrowers at other kids.

Well, except today when Bill couldn't resist short-shooting a lit Ohio Blue Tip between his younger brother Dave's loose-fitting Wranglers and bent-over, exposed butt crack. But a couple of quick follow-up pats prevented injury to person or pants.

August 19 1957: **Embarrassed an enemy to death.**
A dozen of us pre-teen boys gathered for our third and final stealth-and-survival war game of the summer. We marched between a set of railroad tracks to our battlefield, not far south of the city's southernmost street. There, the west side of the grade dropped steeply to a strip of lowland thick with brush plus upright and downed scrub cedars.

We split into two squads, dispersed to opposite ends of the tract, then deployed on solitary seek-and-destroy missions. To eliminate an enemy, you had to spot him before he saw you, then declare, "You're dead." Rules required the casualties to then return to the tracks.

The exercise continued until all of one team's commandos had hit the rails, at which time we'd call winning survivors out of the woods, share war stories and, if time allowed, play again.

The thrill of a "kill" rewarded the painstaking effort it took to surreptitiously crouch, crawl and skulk through the dense, sometimes damp growth. "Dying," on the other hand and as in show biz, was frustrating, disappointing and, especially early in the game, embarrassing.

But no one suffered a more-undignified pretend-end then Palmer (Perry) Moberg. After hearing the clink of a belt buckle, I silently slithered a few yards toward the sound, peered around a moss-covered stump, and spotted Perry. He was squatting over a fallen log, pants and briefs around his ankles, preparing to eliminate. I whisper-shouted, "Gotcha," eliminating Perry. He quickly finished while pleading, "No fair. Shits are automatic time-outs."

"No way, 'cause in a real war you'd be dead," I reasoned, placing Perry on the victim track.

I couldn't wait to brag that I had caught Perry with his pants down and scared the crap out of him. But Perry threatened to beat the crap out of me if I did. I complied, because Perry, who as an adult became a state trooper, was a lot tougher than I.

September 3, 1957: **Left speechless.**

After classmates and I had picked up our seventh-grade schedules, we bemoaned the fact that we were required to take Speech, ruled by Miss Edna Gay Schaaf, who had earned the reputation of being the meanest teacher in junior high.

"You can get out of Speech by taking Band," someone advised. I confirmed at the office, then dropped fifth-hour Speech and added Band in the same slot. After lunch, I reported to the junior-high band director, Mr. Humpal, at Malone Hall, above the auto-repair-class garage in a separate building.

"Do you play an instrument?" he inquired.

When I replied, "Accordion," his first lesson was to educate me that my instrument had no part in either a marching or concert band. But he said the junior-high band needed trumpet players and offered to teach me to play. I agreed, and he handed me a beat-up loaner.

By my senior year, I and a new trumpet purchased with paper-route money had advanced to first chair in the high-school band plus played in swing and stage groups and for pay in a summer concert band sponsored by the city.

September 6, 1957: **Can't be a football hero.**

The only football any of us Queen City boys had competed at was playground touch. So I was excited to try out for the junior-high team and possibly play the real version, with pads, helmet, cleats and coaches. Mom or Dad just had to sign the permission slip I brought home.

Mom declined, stating she was concerned I'd get hurt.

"But I get hurt playing hockey," I argued.

"I can't stop you from playing hockey, but I can football," Mom finalized.

So I went to Dad, who I figured would probably enthusiastically endorse, since he was a former Golden Gloves boxer. But he also said, "No," adding, "you'd end up a cripple."

I knew it would be futile to argue-ask how football could be more damaging than repeatedly getting punched in the face. So my gridiron career ended before it started.

September 10, 1957: **Clean birthday suit required for class.**

I and twenty-some other seventh-grade boys assembled in a large locker room for the first of the mandatory swimming classes we would take weekly for the next five school years. It was common knowledge that we'd swim nude.

But most of us were surprised by the prerequisite hygiene check. Scrutinized by Mr. Michaels, who had also been Dad's junior-high swimming instructor, we scrubbed in a large, communal shower room then single-filed by him. Dad had long ago taught me how to clean myself. Evidently all fathers hadn't, because a few kids failed the inspection and had to repeat shower before jumping into the pool.

September 16, 1957: **Introduced to Queen City-style basketball.**

In gym class, after dribbling and shooting drills, we practiced one-on-ones. Twice, small-but-quick Joey Penoncello burned Roger "Red" Ahola*, who was hereditarily large and pathologically mean. He was also a nurtured favorite of the adult-male athletic establishment, including our teacher, Mr. Olson. He placed his hands on Ahola's shoulders while coaching proper defense, to which the slack-jawed grade-repeater blankly nodded.

---

*Name changed to protect me in case he's still alive and not in prison.

Then when Joey attempted another slick move, Ahola slammed his fist into the little Italian's gut, deflating his diaphragm and loosing the ball. Rolling his eyes and shaking his head, Olson loped past Joey—who had dropped to his knees, gasping for air—to Ahola and exhorted, "No, no, no! In a real game that's not allowed."

Olson then divided us into two squads for a scrimmage, during which I drove the apparently open lane. My clear view of the hoop, however, was quickly obliterated by Ahola's fist coming down sledge-hammer-style. His slam into the bridge of both my glasses and nose sent my eyewear, body, and blood to the hardwood. Olson toweled the floor, stuck a bandaid on my cut nose, then with no admonishment to Ahola, awarded me two free throws. Absent both my corrected eyesight and immediate senses, I didn't even hit the backboard. Adding further embarrassment to injury, I had to tape-repair and wear my glasses classic geek-style until replacement frames arrived.

September 16, 1957: **Hat manners mattered.**

"If you wear hats inside, you'll go bald," Dad once again reminded as a I once again forgot to take off my cap as I entered the house.

While deliberately focusing on the skin roadway that ran between Dad's hair medians, I countered, "Wow, you must have worn hats inside a lot."

"Take it off, smartass," he ordered, while suppressing a smile.

A decade later, during my rejection-of-conventions phase, I wore hats everywhere, including indoors. And not many years later, damn if Dad didn't turn out to be right.

September 21, 1957: **Failed to facilitate fertility.**

Cultivating a worm farm seemed pretty straightforward, according to an article in _Boy's Life_ magazine. So I set out to breed a supply of bait to go after the panfish in Grandpa B's Haenke Lake.

Per instructions, I layered shredded newspaper, well-rotted manure, and vegetable scraps inside a small wood crate. Next, I added some of our garden soil, including a dozen worms, and topped it with a thick book of leaves. I placed the incubator in a basement corner and regularly watered and nourished with coffee grounds, syrup, eggshells, and other recommended food. That, _Boy's Life_ assured, would ensure that my concealed livestock would proliferate.

In late May I dug in, expecting to harvest the first of my crop. However, it quickly became obvious that my "seed" worms had not reproduced exponentially like they were supposed to. In fact, they had likely died and disintegrated before even dating.

October 4, 1957: **Satellite's signal sets my future.**

Russia's sputnik, the first artificial satellite to orbit the earth, launched the space age but didn't immediately impact me. I was unaware that adults in power were institutionally distressed that America had fallen behind in science. I also had given little thought to what I wanted to "be" when I grew up. I just intended to "do" what Dad had consistently encouraged: get an education that would ensure a secure day job.

Four years later, an enthusiastic student-teacher interning in my high-school chemistry class took me aside and said, "You're smart and really have a knack for chemistry. You should become a chemist. Our country needs chemists."

His counsel dovetailed with Dad's, so I became educated as a chemist. And I typed my Masters Degree thesis literally as Neil Armstrong stepped onto the moon.

October 11, 1957: **Good grades were painful.**

As I carried my first junior-high report card down the school stairs, I saw and heard a group of ninth-grade guys laughing and bragging about how many F's they had received. I hoped to pass them unnoticed, but Dennis demanded I hand over my card. He glanced at it then flashed it to the rest. Mike then punched me hard in the shoulder, once for each A I had earned—fortunately for the moment, anyway—two.

The ritual would be repeated, with the number of A's and resultant punches increasing every marking period the rest of the school year.

October 14, 1957: **Dad ordered me to clip him.**

Even though our longtime barber, Fiola the Clipper, charged only fifty cents per haircut, Dad determined it would be more economical to barber at home with a kit from the Sears catalog. The electric clippers and attachments arrived, and Dad immediately cut my hair. I had to admit, his "styling" of my out-of-control cowlicks was an improvement over Fiola's express cut.

Mom then trimmed Dad, which—since he had been patterned bald for nearly ten years* and preferred the strips next to his skin runway to be near-shaved—should have been quick and painless. But Dad uttered too many hair-splitting sidebars about Mom's technique. So she resigned, and he handed the clippers to me. But I didn't feel any pressure, because it was now either me free or fifty-cent Fiola. I flicked a few nicks on my first couple of tries but then performed regular, satisfactory ten-minute cuts until leaving for college six years later. Dad then reunited with Fiola until the Clipper took down his barber pole twenty-five years later.

November 12, 1957: **Got away with serious horsing around.**

While dressing this morning, I shoved my right hand into my pants pocket and the bottom seam separated. I pushed my hand through and touched my knee. As I passed by my dresser, I glanced at my four-inch fixed-blade knife with an orange-resin horse-head handle. Its leather sheath was slit to attach to a belt.

Impulsively, I grabbed a spare leather boot lace, ran it through the opening, dropped my pants, and tied the sheathed blade to my thigh. I then re-hoisted the slacks, with the knife handle poking into my pocket through the tear. I had no intention of doing anything with it. I was just curious what it would feel like to do something illicit.

Initially, I experienced an exhilirating sensation of power and control. But when I slipped my hand onto the horse head as I walked from my locker to class, I near panicked. Unlike elementary school, in junior high we weren't allowed to carry even our fold-up pocket knives. I had no idea what punishment I might suffer if I got caught. I was too young to be forced to join the army. But I could be sent to the reform school at Red Wing. I wanted to terminate my experiment but could not come up with an exit strategy. I was stuck, so wore the worry all day.

Finally at home, relieved, I unhitched the undercover accessory and asked Mom to sew up the pants pocket.

---

*He had actually gone bald before age twenty-two, but his curly, black hair had mysteriously regenerated during his World War II army tour of northern Africa. As a distraction from combat, Dad plotted how to turn the phenomena into a stateside business. During the following two-year march throughout Europe, however, his scheme fell apart when his hair again fell out.

December 21, 1957: **Received a sweet Christmas tip.**

Because of the intensive time and labor required to prepare _potica_ ("poh teet' saw"), the ethnic delicacy was widely prepared only at Thanksgiving, Christmas, Easter, and special family events. Then, mostly at Slavic households, female family members teamed up for days of tedium. They kneaded sweet dough, let it rise, hand-rolled it paper-thin atop the largest available table, then spread a crushed-walnut/sugar/honey/butter mixture over the top. Next— as Charlie described the maneuvers of his mother and aunts—like a baseball ground crew removing a tarpaulin, they rolled layers of sweetness into a long log they then cut into bread-loaf-size sections and baked. Over the next several days, thin slices were shared with relatives and friends.

I got my serving of "Range caviar," as it came to be known, at the Vukolich's, during my paper-route collection circuit. In his thick Croatian accent, grandfatherly Marco greeted me with, "Geddy, Geddy Geddy, please come in and have some of Meddy's (his wife, Mary) _potica_."

December 28, 1957: **The day went downhill.**

Dad's announcement that he'd "picked up a couple of boxes at Hejdas" brought grins to my and Kathy's faces. That meant we'd be headed for a few hours of fun at Eveleth's hilly, snow-covered golf course.

There, we repeatedly rode the thick, reinforced cardboard shipping cartons that had protected console television sets down the slopes. Though the day's high temperature would reach only minus two, the place was swarming with sliders on an assortment of conveyances. Many, like us, hunkered into cardboard boxes. A couple of high-school boys bobsledded on an inverted car hood. Two groups added bounce to their descents on huge "Uke" (Euclid) truck tire inner tubes. One tyke twirled down on a cafeteria tray. And a few families rode actual boughten wood toboggans.

After a couple of dozen slides, my box was literally coming apart at the seams. So I made a final run down the steepest hill. I positioned myself securely as possible into the remainder of my container and pushed off. During the terrifying drop, which appeared to be straight down, my box disintegrated. At the bottom, I clutched only a front-panel remnant.

Trafficking in Skin

W HEN I WAS THREE, Dad hoisted me onto his shoulders as he and Grandpa B headed into the winter woods to, as Grandpa put it, "pick off a few rabbits for dinner."

I expressed only one concern: "Just don't shoot the Easter Bunny."

For the next several winters, I accompanied Grandpa and Dad on pursuits of the camouflaged, but not elusive quarry. Beginning about age seven, I served as a "driver" for Grandpa by tromping naturally noisy through the woods to force rabbits toward him.

When Grandpa spotted a sprinting hare, he bellowed an alto distortion of "Whoopie-tie-yi-yo." That usually brought the startled rabbit to what turned out to be a literal dead stop when Grandpa raised his gun and made a sitting-duck shot. Because Grandpa had lost the sight in his right eye in a mining accident, he sprayed birdshot with his 20-gauge shotgun to guarantee a hit. So when Grandma later prepared hasenpfeffer, we chewed carefully, knowing there'd likely be potentially tooth-cracking BBs we'd have to spit out.

Dad, on the other hand, assigned me to kick brush piles. He'd then stop hares that hopped from those shelters dead in their tracks with a short whistle followed by a clean .22-caliber head shot.

At age nine, I apprenticed while Dad taught me how to snare rabbits. Two years later, I regularly set out solo after the fist-size entrees, which I deposited in our basement chest freezer atop walleye and northern pike Dad had caught, vegetables he had grown, wild berries we had all picked, and a sampler of Grandpa B's homemade sausages.

Plus, I helped pay the way at Walt's Clothiers.

When millions of Eastern European Jews fled persecution during the early 1900s, Ben Walt was among several hundred who settled throughout the Range and opened shops that supplied goods to the burgeoning population of miners. By the time I set my first snare, Mr. Walt had long operated one of the Queen City's dozen and a half apparel stores.

But Ben Walt was the only proprietor who would trade his inventory of manmade wear for the epidermis of just about any wild animal—rabbit, deer, muskrat, fox, weasel, mink, even skunk. We mostly brought in rabbit skins that Dad bartered for socks, long underwear, flannel shirts and wool pants. And after one exceptional snaring streak, I strutted out of Walt's in a new pair of blond-leather Red Wing hunting boots.

Mr. Walt didn't post pelt-price equivalents on his wares, such as "cotton socks—25 cents cash or four prime rabbit skins." No, every transaction involved negotiations that followed the same general script. Unannounced, Dad and I would lug our hides through Walt's alley entrance and flop them onto the wide, worn pine floorboards in an all-purpose back room. The snapping door latch and creaking floor summoned Mr. Walt—a lightbulb-shaped, grandfatherly figure whose thin, white hair swept back under the thin bows of his round, wire glasses. He would solemnly and silently examine our pile for many minutes. We'd then follow him through a set of cafe doors into the sales area where most customers, I supposed, paid actual money for the neatly stacked and racked clothing.

Mr. Walt would then break into a broad smile that exposed his lack of exposure to a dentist, bow slightly, and in a heavy Yiddish accent (he pronounced his last name, "Vault") open with, "Goot eveninK, Howart and," as he patted my head, "handsome, yunk Gary." I took his lie about my looks as a cue to step back and witness the forthcoming commodities exchange.

"Vut do you tink your shkins are vort?" Mr. Walt would query Dad while sweeping his right hand as though offering everything in the store.

Dad would bluster an over-reach like, "Felt boot liners, wool socks, cotton socks, and long-johns for both Gary and me!"

After a couple of polite, smiling nods, Mr. Walt would purse his lips, slowly shake his head as he detailed defects he perceived in our furs, then counter with a lowball, "Two pair cotton shocks, and maybe . . . ahhh, maybe vun pair undervear."

Negotiations then entered a stage of mostly silent staring—Mr. Walt at Dad, and Dad at the floor, with a grimace that revealed an urgent need for a roll of

Tums. Mr. Walt would advance the impasses with incremental upgrades, which Dad would accept, then insist on further concessions as he turned to again silently stare at his floorboard knot. Finally, when it became obvious even to me that Mr. Walt had made his best offer, Dad would signal acceptance by looking directly at Ben while demanding, "Ya gonna throw in a canna boot wax?!"

Mr. Walt would again smile, pluck a tin of Kiwi clear from an end-cap display and the deal was done.

I had no idea what Ben Walt got for our hides or where. All I knew was that his market and, therefore, needs were unpredictable and short-term.

So we regarded rabbits mainly as food. Their pelts might be a bonus. Most winter Saturday afternoons I set snares throughout the scramble of swampland, forest and hills two miles from my back door. And Sunday mornings after church, I collected and cleaned my catches, usually filling my canvas packsack with main courses.

My season ended when snow and rabbits began disappearing—usually around Easter.

Sex Ed

I HAD MY FIRST SEXUAL ENCOUNTER at age four. A more-worldly female, six-year-old neighbor Darlene, predicted in front of my mother that I was going to screw her when we got older. Darlene may have assimilated some understanding of what she had said from her mother, who occasionally and inexplicably postured nude in her doorway in view of Dad as he drove our cows from pasture to barn. I, on the other hand, didn't have a clue. My awareness continued to lag behind learning opportunities.

Soon after Darlene's proposition, for instance, I watched a veterinarian pull on a rubber glove that extended beyond his elbow, then plunge his fist and arm deep into the orifices our cows peed out of. Dad said the man was planting seeds that would grow into calves. I'd rather plant seeds in dirt, I concluded.

That same year, I accompanied Mom and Dad to the hospital to retrieve my new sister, Kathy. A few days later, our minister made a house call. "I know where babies come from," I proudly blurted to him. As Mom leaped from her chair to clamp her hand over my mouth, I finished, "From the hospital. You just go there and pick one up."

When Kathy turned two, Mom insisted that Dad wear pajamas to bed instead of sleeping nude. Mom always wore pajamas, usually layered with a nightgown. But she hadn't cared that I—after sometimes crawling into bed with them in the morning—had seen Dad's bare butt when he hopped out to dress. I wasn't sure why Kathy shouldn't, except she was female. But so was Mom. Confusing.

I also saw Dad and Grandpa Stoltz nude when we took saunas together and, during those steam cleanings, observed that we shared a common appendage. I called my child-size, circumcised model an "acorn." I had never seen a nude human female but, extrapolating my observation of farm animals, sensed that girls were not equipped with acorns.

In kindergarten, I confirmed. Just before our mid-afternoon nap time, classmate Pam wet herself. Miss Gillmor took her into the girls bathroom, where she removed Pam's underpants, rinsed them, and placed them to dry. We then rolled our rag rugs out on the floor and laid down on them. Mine was behind Pam, who was on her back, feet toward me. She spread her legs slightly, and I got an unexpected peek up her dress at what appeared to be an unusual smile. I closed my eyes and turned away.

A year later, I opened my eyes and turned toward. While living in our basement, Mom, Dad, Kathy, infant Reenie, and I slept in a communal bedroom. If I was awake when Mom changed into her nightclothes, she would direct me to pull the covers over my head. One night, curiosity prevailed. What wasn't I supposed to see? I maneuvered the sheet and blankets to create an inconspicuous peephole. Mom's back was to me, and all I saw was her bare derriere. It didn't look much different than Dad's. Spirit of that inquiry satisfied, I never violated Mom's privacy again.

And except for "I see London, I see France, I see someone's underpants" snickers, early elementary school didn't reveal much more about the opposite gender. I never played "doctor." No one claimed to be boyfriend-girlfriend, and few even platonically paired. We boys pretty much stuck to ourselves, and girls reciprocated.

Well, except on Valentines Day, when teachers mandated we give a card to every classmate. So each February, Mom bought an inexpensive packet of assorted generics, with harmless messages like, "Happy Hearts Day" and "Will U B be my Valentine" that I could distribute near-randomly into the large paper folders we had constructed, decorated, and hung from the blackboard tray.

But a couple of cards in each package included overt expressions of "love." Through fourth grade, I had given those to Mom and Grandma B. But in fifth grade, I agonized over whether or not to place one into Cheryl's folder. Cheryl had moved to Virginia and joined our class the year before. She had straw-blond hair, smokey blue eyes, a persistent smile, and quiet, mysterious personality. Oh, man, I was interested in her in a boy-girl way but didn't know what that meant. I decided that dropping a signed expression of "love" into her folder might be a way to start finding out. So did three other boys in our class.

But that didn't deter my enthusiasm. A couple of months later, we took a class trip to the Shrine Circus at Hibbing, twenty-five miles away. While boarding the bus for the return, I maneuvered to sit next to Cheryl. Ten minutes later, I feigned sleep, slowly dropping my head onto her shoulder. The pleasant sensation turned uncomfortable. My neck cramped and my arm fell asleep. Plus, I heard kids snickering. I didn't know if they thought I had actually fallen asleep or whether they knew I was faking and why. Didn't matter. I "woke up" and ended my pursuit of Cheryl, which may have been fortuitous. Six years later, she became pregnant and dropped out of school.

The following summer, I went on my first overnight hike with the Boy Scout troop I had just joined. I didn't sleep well, in part because there was a late, loud commotion down the road from our improvised lakeside campsite. Next morning, the three oldest troop members said they had sneaked out to investigate. Young adults had been partying at a nearby gravel pit, they reported then whispered, "We even saw a used rubber." I pictured a slice of car-tire inner tube, like we used for slingshots or rubber guns, and didn't understand why that merited mention.

A year later, however, my acorn suddenly snapped to attention. It occasionally transformed—at first, seemingly spontaneously—into what I suspected I had heard older boys call a "boner." Then I noticed it seemed to happen when I thought about a female classmate who had started looking really cute. To confirm, I casually lie-blurted to Danny during comic-book trading negotiations, "Boy, do I have a boner."

"Oh yah?" he snickered, "Who are you thinking about?"

That fall, sixth-graders from the Queen City's six elementary schools merged into one seventh-grade class. Included were some seventy-five girls I had never seen before. We rotated classes and classmates hourly, and during the first day, my acorn acted up on the same schedule.

All seventh-graders were also required to take weekly swimming classes. We boys swam in the nude. During one session, as we lined up to practice back dives, I noticed Mike had a boner. He cupped both hands over his embarrassment but couldn't persuade it to droop by the time his turn came. He rushed to the end of the diving board, spun, and back-flopped into the pool. During the maneuver Mike's member pointed at the ceiling as Dave whisper-giggled to me, "Up periscope." I wondered which girl Mike might have been thinking about.

I was also curious if this uncontrollable, sometimes uncomfortable phenomena disrupted adult males, like maybe Dad. I wasn't confident or comfortable enough to ask, but we soon bonded over the subject, sort of. While Mom filed important documents inside the St. Louis County courthouse at Duluth, Dad and I waited in the car. A female like I had never seen in the Queen City grazed our front bumper. The stunning young woman—in retrospect, likely a streetwalker just released on her own recognizance—wore a short, tight black skirt; form-fitting pink blouse unbuttoned to expose four inches of cleavage; black mesh nylons; and stiletto heels. A foot of coal-black hair twisted and twirled atop her head, with cascading wisps shadowing heavily mascaraed eyes. I stared as she near-dislocated her hips walking across the parking lot. Out of the corner of my left eye, I also gauged Dad's reaction. He watched, but expressionless. Then, perhaps noticing my assessment of his assessment, he muttered, "Walks like she's got a frog up her ass." Not sure if that was a put-down or endorsement, I just nodded, relieved that was the end of our talk.

The incident did, however, motivate me to more-closely contemplate the female anatomy, especially the developing bodies of my classmates. I had never seen an exposed female, except for the flash of kindergarten Pam and the butt glimpse of Mom. I had never so much as seen my mother or sisters in their underwear. I hadn't even been allowed to witness my sisters' diaper changes or baths. The Montgomery-Ward catalog did display female undergarments, but not on models. We didn't subscribe to *National Geographic*. I had once seen a naked female mannequin during a Ketola's department store window display change. But her chest bumps were not tipped, which I did know was not anatomically correct. So I didn't bother examining the smooth void between the dummy's legs.

I figured I might solve the mystery by sneaking a peek at one of the girls' swimming classes, conducted in the nude like ours I assumed. I risked a lot of detention inventing an excuse to briefly leave class to one-eye peer through a double-door crack. But the sight yielded no insight. My female classmates wore school-issued one-piece suits that were ill-fitting but not revealing.

I also had never kissed a female, other than obligatory familial pecks, so was nonplussed when confronted with my first opportunity. While walking home after dark, I encountered a group of neighborhood kids, three boys and four girls, all close to my age. They were about to enter a vacant, wooded lot.

"Hey, Barfknecht. C'mon. We need another guy," invited Wilfred.

"Okay," I replied. "What's goin' on?"

I quickly found out. We determined by lottery who would pair up with whom for some boy-girl kissing experiments. Wilfred's sister won me and responded, "Ah, shit, I got Barfknecht."

I mumbled, "Never mind, I gotta go," and left, relieved.

I was still curious but not yet motivated. And at least I now knew that you didn't just go to the hospital and pick up a baby. Three years before, I had observed my baby sister growing in Mom's belly and that Mom had gone to the hospital for help releasing Carolyn before bringing her back home. But I didn't know, hadn't asked, and didn't care how Carolyn got inside Mom's body in the first place. Our church's platitude that babies were gifts God bestowed upon married couples sufficed.

Health and Physical-education teachers didn't deal with the subject. And Mom and Dad weren't proactive. Mom maybe figured, hoped, I would learn the truth about sex the same way I did about the Easter Bunny, Santa Claus, and the Tooth Fairy. Or maybe she mistakenly left it up to Dad, whose sole seminar on the subject was a premature, perplexing, "Make sure you don't *have* to get married."

A TV soap-opera scene, however, advanced my awareness exponentially. After school I'd joined Mom, who was watching *Modern Romances* while ironing. A young, single character sobbed to her mother that she was pregnant.

"Hey, I thought you had to be married to have a baby," I quizzed Mom.

Her head and the iron snapped upright in sync. Mom left the room and—evidently having prepared a backup plan in case I didn't learn on the streets—returned with a pamphlet.

"Here, read this, and if you have any questions, ask me or Dad," she said.

I spent an hour in my room, with the door shut, trying to make sense of the two dozen pages. The comprehensive treatment of the subject matter was clinical, complex, and confusing. But there *was* a black-and-white line-drawing of the female body part I had been most curious about. However, it was disembodied, plus intrusive straight lines connected its curved components to rectangular identifying labels.

Overwhelmed by the geometry and biology, I gave up. Dad had just returned from work and was talking with Mom, who no doubt had unloaded what was unfolding. I sensed they both were terrified I might have questions. So I silently handed the booklet back to Mom. "Did you understand everything," she bravely asked.

"I think so," I lied.

But I *had* gained knowledge. Just not insight. As Rangers liked to counsel, book learning is fine, but hands-on, common-sense experience is more important. For me, the hands-on part would be painfully protracted, because I was too moral, respectful, and frightened to aggressively experiment. But I did learn early on that, when it came to sex, I could count on females to use common sense. Males, not so much.

January 11, 1958: **Dad summed up formal training.**

I could have recited the rules I had learned during a recent gun-safety course. Instead, I violated the most important: Keep the safety on and your finger off the trigger until ready to shoot. And never point your gun at anything you don't intend to shoot.

Dad had motioned me over to dispatch a rabbit he had stopped with a whistle. In my excitement I swung my .22 rifle's muzzle inches in front of his chest as I simultaneously thumbed off the safety and slid my index finger onto the trigger.

The maneuver provoked Dad to shout, "You coulduh f—ing killed me!"

It would be one of the few times Dad raised his voice to me. And it would be the only time I heard him use the "f" word.

Talk about a lesson f—ing learned.

January 19, 1958: **Paid lip service to hockey.**

Usually I only got to watch the high-school-age guys play on our rink. Today, however, they asked me to substitute for the wood snow plow they had placed in goal. I skate-jumped into the opportunity. Minutes later, Keith let go a hard, but long on-the-ice shot that I expected to routinely stick-stop. Instead, at the last second one of my defensemen accidentally deflected the puck directly up into my mouth. Shocked, I reflexively dropped to my knees and examined tiny white pieces of something floating in the red pool that formed in front of me. "Shit, those are my teeth," I exclaimed.

"Nah, Keith reassured, "just ice chips."

As I headed for the shack, I was replaced with the plow and the game resumed. I compressed snow against my bloody, swelling top lip while unlacing and pulling off my skates, then crossed the street home. Dad had taken our car to work, and Mom was bent over the kitchen sink washing her hair. I tapped her on the shoulder and attempted a nonchalant smile. After a few "Oh, my Gods," Mom recruited a neighbor to transport us to the hospital.

There, after a novocaine shot more painful than the puck, a doctor stitched my split upper lip. But no dental work was required. The unexpected frozen snack had only chipped a couple of lower teeth.

February 12, 1958: **Double bonus dining.**

First Covenant's annual "pot luck" supper sometimes was the only time each year we ate out. And it definitely was the only time I looked forward to going to church. The devout parishioners who forsook all other "worldly" pleasures seemed almost normal as we partook of "dishes to pass" placed on folding tables in the church basement. As anticipated, Mrs. Lahti baked her Finnish Cardamom Bread, Mrs. Lanquist congealed a can of creamed corn into Corn Pudding, and Mrs. Nadolske molded orange Jell-O around miniature marshmallows and canned fruit cocktail. And the desert table included Mrs. Richart's Angel Pie and Mrs. Miller's triple-layer Prayer Bars, both of which were reviewed with straight-faced giggles as "sinful."

Most everyone else furnished their permutation of "hot dish"—a can of cream-of-something soup mixed with hamburger and/or vegetable(s) and/or wild rice; topped with cornflake or potato-chip crumbs; and baked in a casserole dish.

February 17, 1958: **No excuse for my excuse.**

Dad was a genius at all things practical and mechanical. But he sometimes expressed regret at ending his formal education at age sixteen to help support his family during the Great Depression. His mantra to me was, "Get an education so you don't have to work in the mines." He reinforced his words by excusing me from chores anytime I had schoolwork.

So tonight, when the thought of spending a frigid hour helping him work on our car sparked a severe bout of teenage irresponsibility, I took advantage of his dispensation. After supper when Dad said, "Let's go," and nodded toward the unheated garage, I exaggerated, "I have a lot of homework to do."

"All right," he said without question.

I watched from the comfort of my bedroom desk chair as Dad headed through the dark, fifteen-below temperature to work alone. I finished my mostly phantom schoolwork and completed my education without ever again malingering.

April 5, 1958: **Good to the last drop shot.**

On a rainy afternoon, Charlie and I competed at coffee-can basketball inside his garage. The hoop was a three-pound Maxwell House tin, bottom removed and serrated top flipped up and nailed by Charlie to the garage door's header. We used a tennis ball to play "round the world" and "horse." Charlie—with home court advantage and more experience and talent—trounced me. Again.

May 19, 1958: **All's well that ends.**

When our scoutmaster found out I played trumpet, he installed me as Troop 121's bugler and handed me a dented, legacy instrument. My only responsibility was to sound taps to close our monthly meetings, held in a basement room at James Madison elementary. Tonight, I was assigned to do same after our annual Court of Honor awards ceremony, attended by parents and other guests.

As the program concluded, I slipped to the far side of an unlit adjoining room, from where I intended to send distant, echoing notes. As scouts saluted and civilians held hands over hearts, Bruce signaled me and I began.

Now, unlike the finger-valved trumpet, the bugle is controlled solely by embouchure. My lips must have cramped, however, because I opened on the wrong note. But I didn't realize it until the second. At the third, I briefly sounded like a bull elk during rut as I searched for the correct pitch. I did settle in tune and finished in the dark solitude, which is where I wanted to stay.

But I emerged to face the music. Adults complimented my perseverance. My friends, on the other hand, weren't so charitable. "Unique arrangement," Charlie giggled. Bruce rubbed his cheek, saying he had broken his face trying to keep it straight. Jim jabbed, "Wow, you really blew that one," then laughed at his pun.

June 28, 1958: **Fantasy camp turned out crappy.**

I convinced three friends to help construct a hidden retreat at what I had determined was a prime site at a secluded bend in Four Mile Creek. Dad's brother Francis owned the property and, even though he and Dad hadn't spoken in years, I convinced myself and coworkers we didn't need permission.

My plan was to dig a section out of the steep bank from its top down to creek level. Within the cutout, we'd construct a one-room log structure—including a short, creekside exit/entry tunnel—and bury it all with the excavated sand and gravel.

On three consecutive afternoons we shouldered picks and shovels on the four-mile round-trip hike to and from the job site. And during each shift, we took breaks to hand-cup drink from the creek. As usual, we only told our parents where we were going and when we'd be back. As usual, none of the adults asked what we were up to. As usual, however, Dad somehow knew.

At supper the night before the scheduled completion of the excavation, as Dad ladled chicken stew onto a soda biscuit he inquired, "So how's the camp comin' along?"

"Fine," I replied, surprised but not enough to blurt details.

"So, where's it at?"

"Four Mile Creek. I think on Uncle Francis's property."

"Yeah, I know where you mean," he replied, ladled again then added, "a mile or so downstream from West Virginia's sewage treatment plant."

Next day I informed my crew that our project was in the toilet.

August 3, 1958: Thought Grandpa had been dismembered.

Grandpa Stoltz had died of stomach cancer, and Mom said we would visit "him" after church. I had never seen a corpse or been in a funeral home. I didn't want to but knew I had to. As I turned the corner into the viewing room, I screamed inside, "Shit, why did they cut off his legs?" As I moved closer, I realized that the lower half of the casket had been closed, exposing Grandpa only from the waist up. Still, he did not look, as Mom had assured, like he was sleeping.

August 27, 1958: Strutted in fabulous footwear.

Snapjack shoes. (Author collection)

I couldn't believe Mom and Dad agreed to buy me a pair of snap-jacks. I figured they'd dismiss the unique shoes as "goofy." Maybe Dad was impressed with the mechanics of the hinged tongue that pulled the sides together on metal track guides then clamped down to hold closed.

Some of my favorite musicians—Eddie Cochran, Gene Vincent, Elvis—wore snap-jacks. Carl Perkins' pair were made of blue suede.

Mine were plain black leather, but I didn't care. For the first time, I wore something genuinely trendy.

September 15, 1958: Counterfeited cool.

I wanted to clack with rebellious panache over our school's marble floors like the hip guys who had nailed horseshoe cleats to the heels of their shoes. But I couldn't afford the heavy metal and knew Mom and Dad wouldn't approve, let alone pay. So on the bus ride to school for a couple of days, I pushed thumbtacks into the bottom edge of my snapjacks' heels, then plucked them out on the trip home. But at school I only clicked, not clacked, so terminated the tacky effort.

September 25, 1958: Debt recovered, dog didn't.

During decent weather, getting paid for delivering newspapers was pretty straightforward. I stood outside customers' doors and yelled, "Collect!" They answered, paid, and I ripped off and handed them tiny, pre-printed, dated receipts from a perforated sheet. Over time, each customer's ledger crept toward the top of my metal flip-binder.

Except for one, a new account that had been added four months before. When I went to collect for the first time, a German shepherd was sprawled over the front steps. When it reared up to launch at me, I lowered my voice and commanded it to get away. But it just sneered, so I left. The dog was always there when I tried to collect, never when I delivered.

But I wasn't concerned about the money. It was a given that everyone in the Queen City paid their bills. Eventually. I knew of small grocery store owners and downtown merchants who routinely allowed customers to charge—based on their word and with no interest—from payday to payday. Most business owners also extended the arrangement during layoffs and strikes. And customers lived up to their word; everyone paid. Eventually. I figured I'd get all that was owed, plus maybe even something extra for my patience. Eventually.

Dad expedited. He asked why the lone page of tabs was sticking down below the others. I explained, and he said, "C'mon." In our garage, he grabbed a scrap piece of two-by-four, and we walked to the delinquent account. As usual, the shepherd rushed while growling, barking, and baring its teeth. I ducked behind Dad, who stood calmly in the street. When the dog crossed the owner's property line, Dad connected its hindquarters with a home-run swing. The stunned shepherd yelped, retreated, and hid behind the house.

I stepped up to the door and yelled, "Collect." The owner answered and paid in full without comment, question or tip. And the dog never bothered me again.

October 1, 1958: **An actual close call with cool.**

We _Minneapolis Tribune_ carriers could earn prizes by signing up new subscribers. After two months of knocking on what seemed every door in town, I had made enough sales to claim the imitation black leather jacked I had coveted. I picked up my prize after our monthly carrier meeting, slipped it on, and walked home, hopeful the vinyl garment might boost me a rung up the cool ladder.

As I turned onto the last two dimly lit blocks to my house, a tenth-grade girl I recognized yelled from the next corner, "Hey, you in the leather jacket, got a cigarette?" Wow, even better than anticipated, my jacket had attracted an older, worldly woman. But I couldn't take advantage. I didn't smoke.

I approached and faked a, "Sorry, I'm out."

She was doubly disappointed, muttering, "Oh, it's you, Barfknecht."

October 2, 1958: **Became a genuine greaser.**

As I pulled my customary peanut butter sandwich from a brown paper bag, Jim and Bruce sat down with cafeteria lunches. Jim spread a pat of butter onto a bread slice, then offered the wrapper to me to lick. I missed the handoff, and the tiny waxed-paper piece dropped and stuck onto my vinyl jacket's sleeve. The rub during the residue removal created a smudge that looked like *real leather*.

Jim and Bruce agreed, so we spent the rest of lunch period coating the coat with butter. Confident that I now really resembled Elvis, I swaggered to my locker and hung up my altered garment. Four hours later I returned, opened the metal door, and was assaulted by a stench remindful of vomit. Rancid butter.

I spared my fellow bus riders the experience by walking home, where I spent an hour restoring the jacket's original patina with soap and hot water.

October 19, 1958: **Lost a friend and faith.**

Jimmy and I suffered mutual boredom during Sunday School, which I guess made us soul mates. So, we sometimes acted silly. During a bathroom break a week ago, for instance, I spit water on Jimmy's pants so it looked like he had wet them. He laughed and promised to get me back.

Yesterday, Jimmy went hunting with a friend who was carrying a 12-gauge shotgun. His companion tripped, and the gun jerked up and discharged inches from Jimmy's head. I had seen what the second most-powerful legal shotgun did to animal flesh and bone. To suppress the image of the blast instantly turning Jimmy's gray matter to red mist, I thought of wet pants and laughter.

Today, our Sunday school teacher preached, "Yesterday, God took one of his children from this class. I was called to pray at his bedside. And just before he went to heaven he said to me, 'I see God.'"

Church now wasn't just boring. It was a lie.

Disordering Foreign Cuisine

WHEN GRANDMA B WON A PIZZA playing a "be the tenth caller" radio game, she assigned her prize to me. I sincerely thanked her, even though I had no idea what she had given me. I had never seen pizza.

When I phoned Rose's Pizza to claim the free mystery food, a female voice congratulated me, then nicely pressured, "Ya get one topping. Whaddaya want—salami, pepperoni, sausage, or hamburger?"

Not knowing what my choice was going to top. I went with the safest known. "Hamburger," I confidently replied.

"It'll be ready in 'bout half an hour. See ya."

Twenty-five minutes later on the cool October night, I pedaled my three-speed Huffy over coarse-cindered, bumpy Twelfth Avenue, one of two links across the swamp to the urban part of town. I then cruised over smooth pavement through Williams Addition to a strip of conjoined, small stores that lined Eighth Street. Black letters on an inconspicuous white vinyl sign attached to the facade of one announced, "Rose's Pizza."

I opened the wood door and stepped into a room not much bigger than and nearly as warm as a sauna. The only furnishing, a chest-high counter held a cash register, phone, pencil, and pad of order forms plus a spindle spiked with the used mint-green slips. A few feet behind, a wall hid the area where I figured pizza was prepared. A toejam-like stench (which I later learned was the "aroma" of Romano cheese) made me breathe open-mouthed. A stout, black-haired woman about Mom's age—Rose, I presumed—shouldered her way through swinging cafe doors from the back room while wiping her glistening brow then hands with the bottom of a once-white apron. "Name?" she asked.

"Barfknecht."

She blasted back through the doors and seconds later reappeared carrying a thin, square cardboard box that she placed on the counter. "There ya go," she said as she skewered my grease-stained order slip onto the spindle then picked up the ringing phone while grabbing the pad and pencil. "Okay, then. Whaddaya want on it—salami, pepperoni, sausage, hamburger?"

Feeling heat as I grabbed the container, I deduced that whatever was inside was supposed to be eaten warm. So I turned my first take-out meal into my first fast food by tucking the box under my left arm, vaulting onto my bike, and speed-bumping home.

There, I opened the box for my first look at pizza. Gravity-glommed into one corner was an amalgamation of what—while forking the mass back over a naked crust circle—I analyzed was cheese, tomato sauce, and hamburger.

I now knew what pizza was supposed to be. And loved it.

Altered States

I SHOVED A DOZEN RABBIT SNARES into my parka pockets and headed out the door to start a typical winter weekend. Nothing about the mild, overcast December Saturday hinted that in a few hours I would be forced to rescue myself and two others.

Mom muttered her standard absent-minded send-off, "Don't get lost," as she closed the door behind me.

"Yeah, okay. See ya later," I mumbled as I set out on the two-mile route to Sun Valley. There, as I had done countless times before, I planned to set my snares by noon, explore new territory, and return just before Dad and dark, both arriving at about 4:15.

But a block from home, Duane and Bobby intruded. "Where ya goin', Barfknecht?" Duane demanded as his floppy-eared, maybe mostly Weimaraner mutt, Silver, cocked his head and made eye contact as though anticipating the answer.

"Settin' snares."

"Okay, we're goin' with," Bobby directed.

Inside, I winced. It wasn't that I didn't like Bobby and Duane. I thought they were good guys, but we had little in common other than living a block away from one another. They were a year younger but tougher on the streets and more talented on the hockey rink than I. Both struggled as students but didn't hold it against me that I didn't. And both had already activated an addiction to cigarettes; I refused to try. But most relevant to the moment, I doubted that either had ever visited the Valley, let alone set a snare. And even if they had, I preferred working solo.

But we set out together and, when out of sight of the city's southernmost adults, Bobby and Duane scratched Ohio Bluetips against their parka zippers and flamed the ends of Luckies. Twenty minutes later as we entered Sun Valley, they made another deposit of carcinogens onto their lungs

We tromped over the wide, straight trail that cut a half mile through woods, brush, and swampland to an extensive ridge that generally and gently serpentined north to south. Along the route, I made short side trips to attach my preformed picture-wire nooses over rabbit runs. Meanwhile, Bobby and Duane whooped and laughed as they lit and flipped flaming birch-bark strips into the air. Silver bounded near-berserk through the snow, suppressing his instinct to flush rabbits to instead satisfy an evidently stronger urge to mark trees. Bobby and Duane did too, by carving their initials into a mature birch. Silver's yellow ink would biodegrade in days. Bobby and Duane's engravings into the white bark would scar black by spring, casting their defacement into stark relief for years.

After I set my last snare, my companions demanded a tour of the area west of the ridge. I reluctantly agreed but, wanting to exit my uncomfortable situation as quickly as possible, advised that we'd better only go the 300 yards I was familiar with to Four Mile Creek then head home. So from the end of the formal trail, we bushwhacked up to the ridge crest then dropped down the relatively open west side to the stream.

As we approached the water's edge, the high, light-gray cloud cover was abruptly displaced by low, black cauldrons that dumped huge, wet snowflakes. But we weren't alarmed. This was no dangerous blizzard. We were warm and dry, the temperature hadn't dropped, and there was no wind. I figured the wet and wild display would dissipate quickly. Several minutes later when it hadn't, I pulled out the railroad pocket watch Grandpa Stoltz had given me. The arrowhead hands pointed to 4:07. The hidden sun was fast dropping below the horizon, and I was past due. Dad and Mom would worry or be mad. Maybe both. I alerted Bobby and Duane, who were splashing snow gobs into the flowing water, that we had just enough light left to sight our way back to the main trail.

Snow now fell so thickly, however, we could barely see past our outstretched arms. Still no problem, I assured a suddenly uneasy Bobby and Duane. We'd follow our earlier bootprints back up and over the ridge to the well-defined corridor out to the road, I instructed. Duane clutched the back of my parka and Bobby grabbed Duane's as we headed home. The impressions from our previous passing, however, quickly faded then disappeared, filled by the incessant downfall. And the white snow now dropped out of blackness. Though I knew this section of my wilderness province like the back of my hand, I could barely see my hand.

I stood paralyzed by a rush of helplessness. I wanted Dad here, now. I was convinced he had been born with an almost supernatural sense of place and direction, an innate, futuristic GPS locater. No matter how deeply we had probed even the most remote, unknown wilderness areas, no matter how frighteningly turned around I had become, Dad had always calmly and confidently led us back to our car. I had no doubt that even through this snowfall thick enough to now obliterate even the darkness he'd know the way. I wished I could be him.

Duane interrupted my descent into despair. "What do we do now, Gary?" He had never addressed me by my first name before.

"Are we lost?" Bobby quavered.

"Nah, I know exactly where we are," I truthfully replied, then thought, "I just don't know how the hell to get out."

Even Silver—haunches sunk into the snow, head again cocked and eyes fixed on mine—appeared to depend on me for direction. "No," I thought with a spasm of hope, "the other way around." Silver, I suggested, could sniff our trail and lead us out. Heck, I had watched Lassie and Rin Tin Tin carry out far more dramatic, complex rescues darned near every week. But in spite of Duane's commands then pleas, the damned dog just spazzed off and back in all directions, stopping only to release phantom drops from his bladder.

Bobby and Duane tried to break the darkness and tension by lighting another Lucky. But the tips of the timber matches they pulled from their parka pockets had turned to blue paste. Wet snow had saturated our outerwear and, as the exterior sog and inside sweat wicked our long johns wet, we began to shiver.

We'd better keep moving, I insisted. But where? We could feel our way up to somewhere on the ridge top. But we wouldn't be able to spot the main trail down through the thick brush on the other side. We could attempt a lucky connection but might instead plunge into one of the many sections of swamp or forest there, so thick and vast we might never find our way out or be found, even in clear daylight. And there was no point in following the crest, since I didn't know where it ended in either direction.

So I led my charges the short distance back to the creek. I knew the water flowed south to Four Mile Lake, a difficult trek under optimum conditions, followed by a mile hike out to Highway 7 and three more miles home.

I had walked north along the creek many times, but only a quarter mile to a camp friends and I had worked on until Dad informed me that a sewage treatment plant discharged its effluent a mile or so upstream. I rejected attempting to follow the water to that facility, because the territory was foreign, possibly impassable. Then I remembered that not far behind my creekside construction site, a strip of woods and brush ended at a large, fallow field. I had only seen it once and didn't investigate. Now seemed the time to try.

My abandoned camp was on the opposite bank, however, so to maximize chances of encountering it, we had to cross the creek. The slow-moving water crawled over our boot tops, soaking and refrigerating our only remaining dry, warm body parts.

Also just then, the distant, rhythmic honk from a car horn snapped our hung heads up. I knew it was Dad. Arriving home through the storm to find I hadn't, he had driven to the Sun Valley trailhead, where he now sounded a locator signal for us. Trouble was we couldn't home in on the faint, echoing beeps precisely enough to risk a blind walk toward them. We were committed.

We plopped our chins back onto chests and close-quarters marched away from Dad's deliverance in search of the spot where coworkers and I had dug deeply into the creek bank. Fifteen minutes later, my abandoned project appeared as a snow-filled swale. We scrambled up alongside, then dead-reckoned our way to the field. There and then, nature and man threw simultaneous switches. Dad stopped honking, snow quit falling, and a light twinkled across the openness. Too tired and weighted to rejoice or run, we silently trudged toward the beacon.

When we reached the lone rural road light, I was thrilled to recognize that the humming fixture illuminated a ninety-degree bend in Mud Lake Road, not far from the farmhouse I had lived in until age five. During my little years here, I had often walked and scootered over the red gravel, sometimes stopping to visit the Pekkalas, a grandparent-aged Finnish couple who I hoped still lived in the house a half block away.

I immediately recognized Mrs. Pekkala when she answered my knock. Since she hadn't seen me in eight years, I politely reintroduced myself. Without volunteering any of the likely obvious details why, I nonchalantly asked if

I could phone home. Probably to keep me from tracking across her gray-flecked, pink kitchen linoleum, Mrs. Pekkala offered to call.

When Mom answered, Mrs. Pekkala—evidently not trusting the lines to carry her voice—yelled, "Lucille? . . . Dis is Synneva Pekkala from da farm. . . . Ohhh, can't complain. You? . . . Good. Hey, listen, Gary and a couple udder kits who I don't know are standin' right here and dey wouldn't mind one-a you guys pickin' 'em up if it's not too much trouble. . . . Well, dey're pretty much soaked ta da bone, ya know, but udderwise don't look too worse for da wear. I tink dey'll live, ya know, ha ha. . . . Ya, Arvid's still runnin' shovel for da Oliver, tanks for askin'. Howard still drivin' truck for Hanna? . . . Hm, hmmm. Okey, dokey, then. Don't be a stranger, now. Bye."

"Your dad's comin'," she said as she placed the black receiver back onto its cradle. I thanked her and excused us back outside to wait.

Dad made it over three miles of barely passable roads in a welcome fifteen minutes. "Everybody okay?" he asked as he opened the doors of our normally boring but now limousine-looking Chevrolet four-door sedan. I repressed an urge to hug him as we all stared at our boots while nodding, "Yeah."

Bobby and Duane slid onto the back seat and I slouched next to Dad in front. As Dad thumbed the tiered pair of heater and fan levers wide open, Duane sobbed, "Silver . . . where's Silver?" Dad stepped out and whistled. The dog sprinted out of the dark and gratefully draped himself over the drive-shaft hump between Bobby and Duane's feet. On the return to Ridgewood, no one interrupted the wooshing heat and Silver's panting.

Pacing silhouettes of anxious mothers faded from picture windows as we dropped off Bobby and Duane. I don't know what happened behind their doors, but when I walked through mine, in a burst of post-traumatic-stress, Mom scolded me for delaying dinner. Then, as Dad settled into his living-room chair with the newspaper, Mom shuttled between warm-ups of supper and me. Soon after, I bid a grateful goodnight and crawled into bed.

As I molded my bedding into a cocoon, Dad appeared bedside. He hadn't yet shaved, and his stubble felt strangely comforting against my ear as he whispered, "You did good, Gar. You got everybody out." I drifted off, too relieved to recognize his pride.

Next morning Mom added what turned out to be the final words ever spoken by anyone about Gary's great misadventure. As I headed out the door to remove rabbits from my Sun Valley snares, she winked and said, "Don't get lost."

No January Thaw

(January 1959 temperatures, Virginia, Minnesota)

	HIGH	LOW		HIGH	LOW		HIGH	LOW
1st	24	-9	11th	28	20	21st	2	-19
2nd-	5	-25	12th	31	12	22nd	3	-30
3rd -	7	-32	13th	31	17	23rd	11	-12
4th	1	-28	14th	17	-8	24th	7	-20
5th	14	-15	15th	-2	-21	25th	10	-22
6th	19	8	16th	-5	-25	26th	22	-7
7th	19	2	17th	13	-18	27th	21	-2
8th	18	-5	18th	8	-16	28th	22	13
9th	23	2	19th	5	-11	29th	17	-17
10th	23	15	20th	5	-19	30th	1	-28
						31st	5	-27

Monthly mean = 1.7°
Average low = -10.5°
Number of nights below 0 = 23
Average high = 12.3°
Number of days above freezing = 0

January 3, 1959: **Momentarily startled, forever awed.**

The radium dial on my bedside clock glowed 5:00 as its alarm ordered me out of bed to deliver the Sunday Minneapolis Tribune. I dressed in layers: cotton long johns under wool pants and shirt; four-buckle rubber boots over felt liners over wool socks; knitted mittens inserted into leather "choppers"; and stocking cap pulled down over my ears and forehead, then encased in a parka hood.

And, since the temperature was forecast to approach forty below zero, I also wrapped and tied two wide scarves—one around my forehead, the other around my nose, mouth and chin—leaving only my eyes exposed. I stacked the papers the distributor had just dropped off onto my sled and set out on my route.

Halfway through, my eyelids blinked shut but didn't reopen. Frost from my breath had deposited so heavily on my eyelashes and lids that they had frozen together. I removed my mitts and pressed my fingers over the ice bond, which melted in seconds.

January 11, 1959: **Game-changing gift.**

Grandpa B handed me an early birthday present, a new Western Field .410 shotgun and a box of Remington Express three-inch shells. I was thrilled, certain the weapon would make me a better hunter. I sometimes missed rabbits with the .22 rifle Dad had given me, because I aimed for difficult head shots so as not to ruin pelts. I was sure the burst of BBs from my new gun would just about guarantee hits.

I set out the next morning to test my theory. As I entered Sun Valley, I snapped the three-shell clip into the .410's belly, slipped a fourth shell into the chamber, and closed the bolt action. Just a few yards up the trail, a rabbit sat just ten yards away. I pointed the .410's sole site bead at it and squeezed the trigger. As anticipated, I scored a direct hit. But the full-choke blast obliterated the potential main course, spattering a Rorschach of red across the snow. Future shots, I realized, would have to be as carefully aimed as the .22.

January 12, 1959: **Criticized for fashion criticism.**

As Mom modeled a new pair of wool slacks she had bought on sale, Dad raved about the heavy material and sturdy construction. "Those'll keep you warm forever," he approved.

I remarked that I thought the nondescript mass of brown fabric made Mom, who was petite and trim, look like a World War I doughboy.

"Wait'll you have to spend your own money on clothes," she snapped. "You'll care about how long they last and not so much about what they look like."

January 16, 1959: **Ran across a salon.**

My normal hairdo was more like a hair-don't. A large cowlick waved up from my forehead, plus stray strands stood at attention elsewhere. And on Fridays, after

The author's 1959 hair don't. (School photo)

spending an hour in chlorinated swimming-class water, my tufts also turned frizzy. I had to douse my scalp with Vitalis to control the chaos.

Today, however, I'd forgotten to bring the tonic, so after swim class I combed my hair into place wet. Then—as the temperature struggled toward the day's high—five below—I ran hatless outside to my next class, band, in a building a block away. En route, my hair froze into an ice wig. I was tempted to try breaking off pieces but didn't.

The styling was temporary. During the hour-long music session, my locks thawed, dripped, dried, and resumed their normal configuration.

February 6, 1959: **Lloyd cooked with an uncommon condiment.**

After school, Dad dropped off Charlie, Bruce, Mike, Lloyd, and me for a "survival" night in rugged territory north of town. Carrying only sleeping bags, hatchets, knives, matches, a bag of white rice, and a metal pot, we tromped to a plateau midway up the lee side of a ridge.

While the others gathered wood and built a fire, I set the snares I had also brought. I returned to a beautiful blaze the guys had lit at the base of a granite monolith. The angled face of the car-size outcropping created a natural draft that drew smoke up and away while reflecting comfortable BTUs. We would have been plenty warm sleeping but, instead, decided to stay up all night and talk.

About 4:00 a.m., our stomachs began growling. So we assigned Lloyd to prepare rice while the rest of us checked my snares. We suspended our cooking pot over the flames and instructed Lloyd, "Melt snow until the pail's three-quarters full. Then when the water boils, dump in the rice."

Half an hour later, we returned with enough rabbits for everyone and Y-shaped willow-sapling spits on which to broast them. Lloyd was hunched over the pot's roiling contents. We circled and surveyed a rice slurry that appeared to have been infused with a grainy mustard. A few of what looked to be golden raisins bobbed on top.

Mike demanded, "Where'd you get the snow for the water?"

Lloyd pointed, "Under that tree."

We moved to a nearby balsam and stared in stunned silence for a couple of seconds. Yellow M&M-size pellets polka-dotted the white beneath the boughs. Damned if Lloyd hadn't scooped snow out of a rabbit restroom. We considered making him taste-test his unique dish.

But without further comment, we lashed the rabbits to the willows with the snare wires and twirled the cuisine above embers. After downing our main courses, we extinguished the remains of the fire with the side dish sewage and hiked out to wait for our ride home.

February 20, 1959: **Cold snap ends**.

After fifty-six consecutive days (December 26, 1958 to February 19, 1959) during which the temperature never rose above freezing, the daytime high finally reached 34°. During the stretch, nighttime lows bottomed out below -10° twenty-seven times, below -20° twelve times, and below -30° three times.

February 21, 1959: **Mike blows up Lloyd.**

During a weekend Troop 121 retreat at Camp Wichingen, Lloyd remained in our cabin while the rest of us took off for an after-supper hockey game on lake ice. We returned at midnight to find Lloyd sound asleep in his lower bunk.

Mike pulled a cherry bomb out of his packsack and speculated it would be hilarious to set it off under Lloyd's bunk. Our scoutmasters were asleep in another cabin, and only Charlie and I lobbied, unsuccessfully, against what we felt was a dangerous stunt.

To embellish the experiment, a couple of guys loosely roped Lloyd—lying on his back, cocooned in his sleeping bag—to his bunk. Mike then lit the green fuse, rolled the pink sphere under the bed, and ran to the rest of us at a far corner. The concussion from the explosion briefly levitated Lloyd against his restraints as smoke billowed up and over him. Lloyd half opened his eyes, raised his head, glanced side to side then, without a word, went back to sleep.

March 12, 1959: **Mail-ordered muscles.**

My free copy of _Everlasting Health and Strength_ arrived from Charles Atlas. For years, I had ignored the images of the barrel-chested muscleman, wearing only

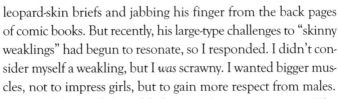

Charles Atlas course before *and* after. (Author collection)

leopard-skin briefs and jabbing his finger from the back pages of comic books. But recently, his large-type challenges to "skinny weaklings" had begun to resonate, so I responded. I didn't consider myself a weakling, but I *was* scrawny. I wanted bigger muscles, not to impress girls, but to gain more respect from males.

Atlas said I could do it without equipment. The forty-eight-page booklet backed him up with testimonials plus before and after photos of successful transformations. All I had to do was send $29.95 for his "Dynamic Tension" course. Then, every two weeks over the next six months, he'd successively mail me twelve illustrated six- to ten-page lessons.

I couldn't afford $29.95. And if I asked my parents for a loan, Dad would likely insist that all I really needed was to do more physical labor. So I tossed the order form and booklet.

Next month, I received a letter from Atlas saying I could subscribe to the course for only twenty dollars. Still beyond my means, so I again ignored it. Over the next couple of months, the solicitations kept coming and the price kept dropping. Finally, I received a final offer. For three dollars, Atlas said he'd send the entire course—text only, no graphics, no diploma—in a single mailing. I gave Mom my paper-route profit for the week, she wrote a check, and two weeks later I received my isometric developmental program.

I asked Kathy to snap a "before" picture of me, then set out to put on pounds of muscle. And over the next year I did grow—taller but without weight gain. So had I bothered with an "after" photo, I would have looked skinnier.

<u>March 15, 1945-1959</u>: **Nighttime lows in Virginia on my birthdays so far.**
+32—1945; +34—1946; -2—1947; +19—1948; +2—1949; +8—1950; +3—1951; +12—1952; +8—1953; +10—1954; -5—1955; +6—1956; +10—1957; +22—1958; -2—1959

<u>April 1, 1959</u>: **Dad faced thirty hard days nights.**
Dad began a brutal month of "shift work." He left for the first of two dayshifts, followed by two midnight shifts, then two afternoons. That was followed

by six days each of day, midnight and afternoon shifts. Dad received premium pay for the exhausting regimen, but had only one weekend off during the month.

But he seized the opportunity because he knew that, with a steelworkers strike looming, there would soon likely be no shifts.

May 10, 1959: **Mom shared her day.**

My sisters and I were thrilled as we scrambled into our Chev for a Mother's Day dinner at one of the area's "supper clubs." We rarely ate out, so this was a special treat for all. Our destination was an unassuming log-sided building tucked into the woods south of the city.

There, after passing out menus, our waitress clanked down an oval glass tray edged with carrots, celery sticks, radishes, olives, and pickles. The vegetable arrangement was centered by a bowl of cheese-spread embraced by a variety of crackers, none of which were Nabisco saltines.

Dad ordered the least-expensive cut of steak but declined the sauteed mushrooms since they cost a quarter extra. Mom requested the Mother's Day special, breaded, deep-fried shrimp. She said we kids could select anything we wanted, "as long as it doesn't cost too much." So I passed on the breaded pork chop topped with a cinnamon apple ring and instead ordered meat loaf and mashed potatoes, both doused with beef gravy that flowed against a dam of canned French-cut green beans.

Desert cost extra, so we returned home and had chocolate cake Mom had baked yesterday.

June 18, 1959: **Left alone for the slaughter.**

Dad arrived home from work and directed, "Everybody outside," meaning he needed major help with something.

I hoped for a quick, typical heavy-lifting assignment. Instead, we got choreographed chaos.

On our garage's concrete floor, three gunny sacks writhed, cackled and squawked. As Mom, my sisters, and I apprehensively glanced at each other, Dad recounted that he had spotted a farmer's hand-scrawled sign offering live chickens for nineteen cents a pound. Such a deal he couldn't pass up, so he stuffed the burlap bags with bargain birds that he directed we would now "dress."

He then set up what he intended to be an efficient assembly line operation. I held the first chicken upside down by its feet while Dad opened its beak, stabbed a knife back into the birdbrain (an unconventional terminating technique he claimed made feather removal easier), then slit its throat. Kathy positioned a bucket to catch the red flow. The fowl also evacuated its bowels and, while reflexively flapping, splattered us with blood and yellow-gray feces.

Next, Reenie dunked the carcass into a tub of hot water, then we all plucked the body close to clean. Mom singed off residual hairs with wood matches then flipped the bird back to Dad. He made a quick incision, eviscerated the fowl with his fingers, then cleavered off its head and feet. And finally, Mom rinsed the naked, disemboweled amputee in ice water, stuffed heart, gizzards and liver back inside its body cavity, and wrapped and sealed the future meal in white freezer paper.

As Dad again reached into the bag, Mom and my sisters—sensibilities stunned—left en masse, leaving me to multitask.

July 3, 1959: **Uncle explained alternate use for female equipment.**

During one of his infrequent visits from "the cities" (Minneapolis/St. Paul), Dad's lookalike brother, Cliff, and I watched the Virginia women's fast-pitch softball team practice. Many players had muscular bodies, short-cropped hair, names like "Pushka" and "Squeegee," and played ball better than any male in our neighborhood.

Evidently I now looked worldly enough for Uncle Cliff to whisper, "They're queer, you know." Then, recognizing my otherworldly expression, he added, "You know, they like other women, not men." I vaguely grasped the new concept but didn't know how to respond. So I just nodded.

August 3, 1959: **Ashes to ashes, rust to rust.**

Automobiles were constructed almost totally of steel, which was processed from Range iron ore. Range cars were also colored the same—rust red. Oh, some arrived displaying other hues, but ubiquitous ore dust quickly and relentlessly veneered them and just about everything else iron red.

Terminally inoperable vehicles were recycled as parts or scrap metal. When farm vehicles and implements were no longer able to perform, however, they were often simply put out to pasture.

Today, during a milk run to the Hellyer farm, I contemplated scattered, deteriorating relics that had been abandoned in the fields decades ago. They were, it struck me, returning from where they came. Iron ore from the Range was ferrous oxide—rust.

August 14, 1959: Uncle almost became punchline to his joke.

Uncle Wilson Barfknecht met up with a fishing buddy, who had also invited an eighty-year-old neighbor. Wilson and the stranger were quickly introduced by first names only. The trio then headed by boat out onto an expansive Lake Vermilion bay. En route, while Wilson's buddy ran the noisy motor, my loquacious uncle regaled the taciturn old man with a series of Finnlander jokes. (For reasons too esoteric to go into, of the forty-plus immigrant groups that had settled the Range, Finns had become the butt of most ethnic jokes.)

He concluded with:

Q: "Why can't you bury Finnlanders at sea?"

A: "Shit floats."

The old-timer, who had stared into the lake silent and expressionless, turned, glared, then growled in a heavy, first-generation Finnish accent, "Parfneck, weer tree miles from shore and you ain't Cheesus Christ."

August 19, 1959: Idled miners not idle.

During a thirteen-week-long mine layoff due to a steelworkers strike, Dad and other neighborhood men began construction of a "community center" to replace our small, crude ice-rink warming shack. A month later, using donated materials from area businesses, the men completed the ranch-style structure, which included a kitchen and bathrooms.

Subsequent use of the building expanded to include children's summer programming, arts and crafts shows, and other activities. However, even today, everyone in the Queen City—including *Mesabi Daily News* announcements—still refers to the venue as "the Ridgewood shack."

August 27, 1959: Mom placed a tall order.

During the summer prior to my final year of junior high, my perspective changed. Literally. After resigning myself to the fact that I was always going to remain one of the shortest boys in my grade, I shot up to five-foot-seven, which placed me near the top of my class.

Coincidentally, Mom purchased my first-ever sport coat, on sale from the Sears Catalog. It arrived today and I tried it on. Mom evidently expected me to top out as a typical Barfknecht male, around six feet, because the coat was two sizes too big. "Looks good," she said, "and I love the colors and pattern."

To me, the maroon, cream, and black plaid made me look like I was wrapped in a Nash Rambler seat cover.

Several times over the next four years, I reluctantly wore the garment. But I never grew into it.

September 8, 1959: **Catholics add to our class.**

Queen City Catholics supported three churches: St. Mary's, on the north side, and Our Lady of Lourdes and (Polish) St. Johns, near downtown. Marquette Parochial School stood between the latter two. Nuns there taught only grades one through eight, however, so students had to transfer to public school at grade nine.

Our class's influx included an Italian tough guy who fought our reigning Nordic alpha male for the distinction. The after-school bout was a consensus draw.

I singled out a cute girl, who didn't know me well enough to reject me out of hand. It took a week.

September 13, 1959: **Church lady again tried to exorcise Satan from sports.**

Miss Korpy, one of our church's pillars and longtime high-school English teacher, renewed her annual, passive, brief and unsuccessful campaign to change the name of our high-school mascot, the "Blue Devils." Since our Roosevelt High was named after President Theodore, she advocated the "Teddy Bears."

September 20, 1959: **Discovered fame is elusive.**

During an interview with Mom's mother, Grandma (Grace) Sukow, for a school family-history project, she proudly and accurately declared that John A. Johnson—Minnesota's sixteenth governor and the first to die in office—was her mother's first cousin.

She also told me that, as young marrieds, she and Grandpa (Edward) had lived near Buffalo Bill Cody's sister in West Duluth (also true, I verified decades later) and that they had seen the wild-west showman visit there.

I revealed my many degrees of separation to the teacher and class, but few believed me. And no one cared.

October 14, 1959: **Is this the party to whom I'm speaking?**

I needed to ask a classmate an important homework question. I knew the boy was visiting his first-generation Finnish grandfather, so I called there. The man answered, "Dis iss me. Hoos you?"

<u>November 1, 1959</u>: **Dad passed along a bit of firearms wisdom, the value of which still eludes me.**

While walking the woods, I heard a bullet whistle by and thunk into the trunk of a large birch about ten yards away. I didn't see the shooter, and presumably he hadn't seen me. I told Dad about the near hit. He nodded, then solemnly imparted, "As long as you hear it, you got nothin' to worry about."

<u>November 21, 1959</u>: **Learned how to dress defensively.**

Hardly anyone made the varsity hockey team as a ninth-grader, but I tried out anyway. I wanted Mr. Beste, the coach, to get a look at me, maybe assign me to the junior varsity (JV) team, and possibly promote me to varsity next season.

I waited near the end of the line in the Ewens Field clubhouse as the lettered veterans got their gear from musclebound Mr. Moehlenbrock, staff equipment manager for all sports. When my turn came, the serial weightlifter grabbed a cup, shoulder pads, shinguards, elbow pads, pants, socks, garter belt, gloves, practice jersey, and helmet from the shelves behind and handed the pile to me. Though I had played hockey almost every frozen day since age six, I had never worn protective equipment and didn't know how to put most of it on. I moved to a back bench to watch and copy the older guys.

Mr. Beste then ordered us out onto the natural ice rink set up on the school's cinder running track, which was also the baseball squad's left-field warning track, near the football team's end zone. For the next hour, coach Beste assessed our skills through a series of demanding drills. While showering afterward, pairs of older players grabbed each of us rookies by our hands and feet, opened the clubhouse door, and slung us into the snow. After the initiation, Mr. Beste entered the locker room, gathered several new tryouts into a group, and told them they needn't return the next day. I wasn't included and continued practicing through the week.

On Saturday, Mom dropped me off for a morning practice, during which she grocery shopped at the Red Owl supermarket, nearby. Before the drills and scrimmage, Mr. Beste said he'd decide final cuts after the session and post a list outside the athletic director's office on Monday. As expected, I was on that list. But as hoped, my name *was* included on the JV roster. I didn't have to turn in the suit of armor I had become accustomed to wearing. Plus I was one of three JV players selected to clean the outdoor ice with plows and shovels between periods of the varsity's home games.

Out of Place, In Time

B₀ϐ ZIMMERMAN AND I GREW UP together separately on the Range. He was raised in Hibbing, "Iron Ore Capital of the World," twenty-five miles from my "Queen City of the Iron Range." As boys, we both played hockey. And we both took to music early. I became a virtuoso at the Mesabi's national instrument, the accordion. Bobby changed his last name to "Dylan" and went in a different direction.

Bob Dylan is a striking Range anomaly. The Mesabi is not known as a breeding ground for artists of any genre. You could count on the fingers of one hand of a really careless miner the number of widely recognized actors, painters, musicians, writers, sculptors, or other creative types who have come out of the Range. I can recall only one other, Frances Gumm, from Grand Rapids, who also changed her name, to Judy Garland.

Range adults had little interest in pursuits that didn't produce utilitarian results. Reason was, pragmatism was the primary weapon in their common defense against the certainty of cold and uncertainty of an existence dependent on mining. Uniformity was their bond of reassurance. And coercion to conform was subtle but pervasive.

In fact I hadn't felt it as a kid. Range life had been a comfortable fit. Now in my my early teens, however, I sensed pressure to metamorphose into an adult Range male. The concept was unsettling. I was eager to become a man, and my model should have been Dad. But we were so different. Dad didn't have an artistic bone in his body, and I felt like I hadn't been endowed with even a little finger's worth of practicality. To me, Dad was a hands-on deity. He possessed a seemingly inherent understanding of everything mechanical.

145

There was nothing he couldn't repair and little he couldn't build. He always knew what to do, he was never in doubt, and he never made mistakes. And I figured he'd been that way since he was nine. I wasn't like him, knew I never could be, and worse in my conflicted teen mind, didn't want to be. Not only did I feel defective, but like I was rejecting, even betraying Dad.

But Dad himself applied no direct pressure. He encouraged my endeavors, even the schemes he didn't comprehend. And his support was unqualified. He did, however, consistently offer unsolicited practical advice, particularly pointing out my often-convoluted, impractical techniques. And when he got totally frustrated watching me "putz around," he'd take over and finish quickly and directly.

But to me, the process was the pleasure. The end meant the means was over. Maybe that's why I didn't care about streamlining the means. Or maybe I had inherited my lack of instinct and enthusiasm for things practical from Mom. Whichever or whatever, the likelihood of my becoming a certified adult Range male was less than that of a January thaw.

School curriculum, however, mandated that I try. Starting in seventh grade, my brethren and I were required to take practical "industrial arts" classes an hour every school day for the next two years. Creative visual arts was scheduled one hour a week. I earned A's T-squaring blueprints in Drafting and setting movable lead type in Printing. For B's, I wired circuits in Electricity and crimped tin into almost-usable objects in Metalwork. I received a compassionate C in Woodturning, where I once sent classmates into duck-and-cover mode by launching a "spinner" off my lathe. And I passed Forge, even after absentmindedly superheating a chunk of solid iron into a "sparkler." Twice.

I was supremely grateful that Auto Mechanics was elective. Vehicles transcended function on the Range. They were the third most-common topic of conversation, behind only mining and politics but ahead of weather. To be considered a bonafide Range male, I would have to conduct regular headlight-to-tailpipe exams, diagnose maladies, perform corrective surgery or even transplants, and issue intake and exhaustive reports. But I had no aptitude and a bad attitude.

I had, however, performed well and with enthusiasm at a few other male-sanctioned pursuits. I was good in the woods, I was on a fast track to becoming the city's youngest-ever Eagle Scout, and I had donated my body to hockey.

And I excelled at music, the lone art form not only appreciated but encouraged in the Queen City. Which puzzled me. I didn't see a utilitarian connection, so didn't understand what adults got out of music that they couldn't from other artistic expression. Maybe it wasn't a matter of choice. As researchers would later speculate, maybe all humans come into the world musically hard-wired.

If so, I had been issued with a circuit breaker that wouldn't overload. I crashed cymbals in my kindergarten band and belted out patriotic songs in grade-school music classes. I stacked Mom's World War II-era 78s onto the spindle of her Silvertone record-player/radio combo. I spent my paper-route money on an entry-level 45-rpm record player with a stylus I had to weight down with a taped nickel to hear "Bye Bye Love" and "Peggy Sue" non-skip. I devoured whatever music WHLB radio broadcast, from Bobby Aro's Finnish-accented silly songs to, finally and gratefully, a half hour of *Teen Time*. And my TV must-watches included *Hit Parade*, *Name That Tune*, *Liberace*, and a Duluth-station, after-school version of *Bandstand*. In a couple of years, I would perform solo and in groups on the accordion; play trumpet in concert, marching, and dance bands; dabble with drums; and teach myself guitar well enough to play underage in a bar band.

I was also successful at school, which was endorsed to a point. Adults appreciated and encouraged educational achievement in the basic "three R's" but saw little value in abstract, conceptual, or academic thought or expression. Anyone regarded as overtly intellectual was dismissed as being, "smart, but no common sense."

I suspected the pejorative praise might be whispered about me some day. I recognized that my perceptions rarely paralleled, let alone intersected, those of other Rangers. Plus, my greatest pleasure came from changing or bringing something new into my world daily. Range adults, it seemed, were forced into living the same way, day after redundant day. I was becoming an uncomfortable fit, maybe misfit.

I had little idea what lie beyond the Range but felt driven to find out. I set my sights on college at the University of Minnesota as a start.

I did leave. I did earn a University of Minnesota diploma. And I did become a man. Not a Range man, but enough of one to help me make it on the outside.

On my own. But not alone.

Epilogue

The Spirit of Mesabi

As a kid, I assumed the name of our iron range, "Mesabi," was American Indian; it sounded like Tonto's "Kemo Sabe." I gave it little thought until I later learned "Mesabi" was indeed Dakota for "giant." I looked at a sketch of their Mesabi—lying on his left side, knees drawn up, arms folded as though asleep.

But to me, even outline maps of the iron ore deposits that defined our region didn't resemble Mesabi's figure enough to be given his name. Besides, how could the ancient Dakota possibly have known the mineral was even there, I wondered. They hadn't. The legend of Mesabi, as I heard it, transcended the red rock.

Mesabi *was* a giant—standing taller than the clouds. He traveled the great north from the beginning of time, gathering, hiding, guarding treasures. He persevered for eons, then lay down for eternal sleep. His immense form slowly transfigured into a contour of ridges and hills. Trees then covered Mesabi, and his footprints filled with water. He had reposed so rain that fell on him flowed to three great water bodies—the Atlantic Ocean, Gulf of Mexico, and Hudson Bay.

When the Dakota first encountered the formation, they called it Mesabi-Watchu, "big man hills." Mesabi's lakes, rivers, woods, and wildlife sustained them. Europeans arrived, trapped animals and sold their pelts. Americans followed, stripping off Mesabi's white-pine blanket. Others searched for gold, but he had hidden little. A fortunate few, however, discovered his most valuable treasure, iron ore.

By the time I was embraced by the sleeping giant, his name had come to identify not only our distinct geographic region but also the singular, closed culture that had evolved within. We Rangers were rightly reputed to be endowed with a distinctive, provincial strength and independence. And, yes, quirkiness.

I purposefully and permanently left the Range. But I was deeply imprinted by the Range and still consider myself a Ranger. And I sometimes miss Mesabi. Especially—incomprehensibly to most, sometimes even to me—the winters.

About the Author

H<small>I, I'M</small> G<small>ARY</small> B<small>ARFKNECHT</small>.

About my last name. It's German. My genetic grandfathers, both of direct Deutsch heritage, made sure I knew that. But they didn't tell me what "Barfknecht" translated to in English, probably because they didn't know. For many years, neither did I.

My friends called me "Barf," which also had no further meaning until eighth grade, when a high-school neighbor guy who drove me to and from our band events teased, "Wow, you have a great drinking name." I asked what he meant. He explained.

In college, while taking my first German class, I looked up "knecht" in a German-English dictionary. The first translation was "servant." "Barf," however, was not listed. But, fortuitously, I worked in the dorm cafeteria with Martha Grue, a diminutive German-immigrant cook. I asked her, "Can you tell me what 'barf' means in English?"

"Ya, sure," she answered, "it's short for 'barfuss,' which means 'barefoot.'"

So I'm Gary Barfknecht, barefoot servant from the Queen City.

Gary W. Barfknecht, sixty-nine, was born and raised in Virginia, Minnesota, the "Queen City" of that state's Mesabi Iron Range. After receiving a Bachelor of Science degree from the University of Minnesota in 1967 and a Master of Science degree from the University of Washington (Seattle) in 1969, Barfknecht came to Flint, Michigan, as a paint chemist with the E.I. DuPont & deNemours company.

But after a year on the job, Barfknecht and the chemical giant reached the mutual conclusion that he was not suitable for corporate life, and Barfknecht set out on a freelance writing career. Over the next several years, his articles were featured in national publications.

While freelancing, Barfknecht also managed a hockey pro shop at a Flint ice arena. That job led to a position as hockey commissioner. In 1977 Barfknecht postponed his writing efforts when he took over the directorship of almost all amateur hockey programs in Michigan's fourth-largest county.

He resumed his writing career in 1981 with the release of *Michillaneous*, a critically acclaimed, best-selling collection of Michigan trivia. In 1983 Barfknecht followed with *Murder, Michigan*, which described "the dark side of Michigan history." Over the next eighteen years he followed with six more Michigan-themed, non-fiction books: *Mich-Again's Day, Michillaneous II, Ultimate Michigan Adventures, Unexplained Michigan Mysteries, The Michigan Book of Bests*, and *39 Petoskey Walkabouts*.

As sole proprietor and managing editor of Friede Publications, Barfknecht also brought eighteen books by other Michigan authors into print.

During the summer, Barfknecht resides with his wife, Ann, in Petoskey, Michigan. In winter, they relocate to Alexandria, Virginia, near their two daughters, husbands, and five grandchildren.